D0517375

PATH:
A Career Workbook for Liberal Arts Students

by

HOWARD E. FIGLER
Director of Counseling and Placement,
Dickinson College

Drawings by GORDON BROOKS

First Edition

THE CARROLL
PRESS
Publishers

43 Squantum St., Cranston, R. I. 02920

6.25

About the Author

Howard E. Figler is a counseling psychologist whose special interests are in career development for college students and the building of outreach models for school and college counselors. He is currently Director of Counseling and Placement at Dickinson College and has also served as Counseling Psychologist at the University of Tennessee at Chattanooga. Prior to his work with college students, he was a research grants administrator for the U.S. Office of Education and did personnel work with the Prudential Insurance Company and the Port of New York Authority.

Dr. Figler is the author of numerous articles on career counseling. His article entitled "Job Satisfaction and the Need for Life Counseling" was named as the best article for 1972 in the *Journal of College Placement.*

With David J. Drum of the University of Rhode Island as the co-author, Dr. Figler wrote *Outreach In Counseling* (1973), the first text dealing with outreach models in the counseling profession. He and Dr. Drum are co-authors of numerous articles on this topic.

Dr. Figler earned his Bachelor of Arts degree in Economics and Mathematics at Emory University, a Master's of Business Administration at New York University, and a Ph. D. in Educational Research and Testing from Florida State University.

About the Artist:

The Brooks name is already well-known to Cape Cod residents and visitors from the lively cartoons which have appeared in the weekly *Cape Codder* under the caption, "Brooks Looks," and for the "Brooks Cards" imprint on the line of greeting cards he designs and manufactures at his home shop in Brewster, Mass.

Gordon Brooks is a graduate of Clark University and the School of Practical Art in Boston. As a commercial artist, he worked for advertising agencies and publishers on all kinds of assignments including animated cartoons and comic books.

Library of Congress Cataloging in Publication Data

Figler, Howard E.
  PATH: A career workbook for liberal arts students.
  Bibliography: p.
  1. Vocational guidance. A. Vocational guidance—Problems, exercises, etc. I. Title.
  HF5381.F477   331.7 02   74-12041

ISBN 0-910328-07

Cover design by Julius Spakevicius, Boston, Mass.

Manufactured in the United States of America

PATH
A Career Workbook for Liberal Arts Students

My life describes a path; its way may not be straight, but it has direction; it may not be predictable, but it responds to the changing pattern of my needs; it may not seem entirely logical to you, but it makes perfectly good sense to me.

CONTENTS

*Core Program

CONTENTS

— continued —

*Core Program

PREFACE

If you are a liberal arts student and are one-half the person you think you are, you want a job that involves: (a) helping people; (b) building a better society; (c) a lot of change and variety; and (d) the opportunity to be your own boss.

Your parents will remind you that idealism is nice for those who can afford it, but it doesn't pay the rent. And remember, "You will want to live in the style to which you have become accustomed." But, you insist, the fast buck is a trap, and those who forget the lessons of the past are doomed to repeat them.

So, instant riches are not important to you, and you are willing to forego the key to the executive washroom. You would like to try something new, experiment, be daring, risk failure, even make a fool of yourself, as long as you can avoid the boredom which haunts so many of the older people around you.

But then, you hear these awful stories about liberal arts degrees being a dime a dozen, and graduates having to settle for whatever job comes their way, whether it's hash house cook, insurance clerk, or department store floorwalker. What's a person to do?

You must turn this career process around so that you are in charge of your life rather than being the victim of employers' whims. This initiative will not come easily. You have to know who you are and what you want to get from your working life. The exercises in PATH, if you complete them with patience and self-honesty, will put you on the trail to self-fulfillment. At the end of the program, you will know a lot about what you most want to do with your life and will have a pretty good idea of where to find it.

I have no illusions that PATH will make any life-long decisions for you because your life (like mine) will be in a constant state of change. Nor do I expect that it will reveal any deep, mysteriously hidden dimensions of your being because you probably know yourself pretty well by now.

However, I do expect that PATH will give you a clear picture of your values priorities and a firmer grasp upon those talents or abilities which come naturally to you. It will also help you to see that your life priorities and your work priorities can have a lot in common.

Most of all, I hope that PATH teaches you to regard your career as an endeavor in which you must invest a great deal of yourself, and that your investment will be the greatest if you choose work that you enjoy very much and do especially well. If the PATH Program succeeds in this, it will have done its job well indeed.

HOWARD E. FIGLER

Carlisle, Pennsylvania
December, 1974

ACKNOWLEDGEMENTS

In the process of developing the PATH program, the author has drawn ideas and inspiration from the work of several key individuals.

Several years ago, the work of Gerald Halpern and Martin R. Katz at the Educational Testing Service provided initial impetus for the author's conceptualization of career development programs. More recently, the DIG (Deeper Investigation of Growth) Program developed by Richard Gummere at Columbia University has helped the author to develop ideas about the analysis of an individual's positive, career-related attributes. Most recently, the author owes a debt of gratitude to Richard N. Bolles and John Crystal. Bolles' book, What Color Is Your Parachute?, influenced the author greatly in the development of an individual-centered approach to career development. Bolles' and Crystal's methods have been published this year in Where Do I Go From Here With My Life? Also, the author's emphasis upon self-recognition of values was nurtured by the writing of Katz (Decisions and Values) and Sidney Simon, Howard Kirschenbaum, and Leland Howe (Values Clarification).

The author recognizes that, without the conceptual nourishment that has been provided by the above-named individuals and their published works, he would not have been able to develop the PATH program.

After the first draft of the manuscript was completed, Dr. David Drum was kind enough to read it several times and suggested major revisions of the text and program.

Grateful appreciation is offered to Dottie Wolfe who has typed the seemingly endless revisions of this manuscript during the past three years, offered timely criticism, and has taken it all with good humor and cheer.

Section I:

PRINCIPLES of the PATH PROGRAM

The PATH Program is a modest attempt to meet a need of the liberal arts college student which has long been unanswered — a simple, yet workable way to develop career objectives. PATH is a self-instructional workbook which is designed so that you can answer the following questions:

1. What do I like to do best and can these things be a part of my career?

2. What are my values and how do they relate to a career?

3. What are the most prominent skills and talents that I can offer to a career?

4. What do I most want to accomplish in my work life?

5. What can I do during college to get my career process underway?

6. How do I find the people who are doing the kinds of work that I would most like to do?

In many ways, the liberal education makes it very difficult for you to generate a career objective: (1) Most academic coursework is decidedly non-vocational; (2) Most professors view graduate school in their own disciplines as the most desirable route to follow after graduation; (3) The liberal education raises your enthusiasm for many fields of study. In the curious, but illogical way that students link academic fields to vocations, this expanded enthusiasm tends to increase your number of vocational possibilities and thus further confuses you when you are trying to focus upon a career objective; (4) There is little concern for your vocational indecision reflected within the liberal arts curriculum; (5) In those places where you can find someone who wants to help (i.e., a faculty advisor, a career counselor, or a placement official), there is seldom any systematic method available which you can use to develop a career objective that will represent reliably your strongest needs and most prominent talents. Testing methods and other approaches are widely available, but it will be argued that these methods do not validly represent the individual's total needs and thus can often lead to faulty career decisions.

The PATH Program offers a solution to this muddled state of affairs for the liberal arts student in the following ways:

1. By working through the program from beginning to end, the individual will obtain specific career objectives;

2. The program informs you every step of the way about how your career objectives are being developed and the factors which contribute to them;

3. The program takes account of every field of work that interests you and incorporates these into the development of your career objectives;

4. Your career objectives are comprehensive because they bring together all of your strongest needs and capabilities and allow you to include them all, rather than being forced to select some priorities and discard others.

This workbook can be used profitably by both liberal arts graduates and students who have not yet completed their education. If you are still in college, you should be aware that the earlier you use the PATH Program, the more likely it will benefit you. It is important to get your career exploration underway as early as you can before other critical life decisions (marriage, etc.) compete for your attention. It is particularly important to think about careers before your economic independence becomes a necessity. That is, when you find that you must have a job, the career exploration process is compressed and necessarily a hurried one.

Ten Myths About Career Decision Making

The following myths about the career decision making process need to be exposed and exploded before you can apply yourself seriously to the problem:

Myth No. 1: The major field of study predicts the career of the liberal arts graduate.

On the contrary, most liberal arts majors are not vocationally specific; hence the greater proportion of liberally educated people find themselves choosing work which is not directly related to their major field of study.

Myth No. 2: A liberal arts graduate is nothing without a graduate or professional degree.

On the contrary, many thousands of liberal arts graduates are prominently employed in business, social service, government, publishing, and elsewhere, without having acquired advanced educational credentials.

Myth No. 3: A liberal arts graduate must have experience to find a job.

On the contrary, as a new college graduate, you are hired primarily for your potential to learn and advance within the organization rather than for your existing work capabilities or experience.

Myth No. 4: There is little opportunity for a liberal arts student to explore careers.

On the contrary, there are methods which you can use outside of the classroom (during college) to investigate career possibilities, and these methods do not require special vocational knowledge.

<u>Myth No. 5</u>: Most people start their careers at about age 21 and proceed in a straight line toward their ultimate career objectives.

On the contrary, the career paths of most people are filled with zigs and zags, and sudden changes of direction. People do not reach their ultimate career decisions when they are 21 because the experiences they gather in one type of work change their attitudes about careers and have application to many other kinds of work (e. g. , news reporting and interviewing can be adapted to later work in social service, management consulting and public relations).

People are seldom aware of the extent to which their past job experiences gave them flexibility in pursuing future jobs and the degree to which these experiences acted to change their career needs. But this versatility is openly expressed in their own career paths. There are social workers who have become city planners, advertising writers who have become management consultants, mortgage loan brokers who are now magazine writers and so forth.

Ask people who are 35 what they were doing when they turned 21 and you may be amazed to discover that, in many cases, they were doing work that was worlds apart from their current job. And these people will say, "I just had a lucky break. " They are unaware of the inherent fluidity of the career development process, the degree to which their own needs change through experience and the ways in which their past experience is used in their present jobs.

<u>Myth No. 6</u>: Career planning is an irreversible process.

On the contrary, you can change career directions whenever your talents and needs dictate, because these attributes are in a continual state of being changed and reshaped by vocational experience.

<u>Myth No. 7</u>: A liberal arts student has few talents which are valuable in the world of work.

On the contrary, by the time you are 18 or 20 years old, you have developed identifiable abilities that can be applied successfully to a wide variety of occupations.

<u>Myth No. 8</u>: There is one right job for me.

On the contrary, you are multi-potential. There are numerous job situations in which your talents can be equally applied and the nature of these possibilities will expand as your work experiences accumulate.

<u>Myth No. 9</u>: Each and every job requires a particular set of talents.

On the contrary, most jobs except highly technical and specific ones, can be accomplished in a variety of ways, by people who possess different sets of capabilities.

Myth No. 10:   There is a particular set of job responsibilities for every
occupation.

On the contrary, people in positions having the same title are very often
performing different tasks or performing similar tasks according to very
different styles. Very often their job responsibilities differ because of
the varying capabilities of the people who inhabit the positions.

Should I Go Directly to Graduate School?

Graduate school has become the trade school of the liberal arts graduate.
You may feel it is your answer to the increased demand for "specialists" in our
economy. For many areas of work, the value of a specialized education cannot
be denied. However, the liberal arts graduate must be careful not to make this
leap into specialized study before he or she has a thorough understanding of his
career objectives.

It is perhaps truer than ever that many liberal arts students may regard
their undergraduate years as training for advanced education in law, medicine,
business or some kind of master's or doctoral program. This can be a dangerous
mind-set because —

1. There may be only a tenuous relationship between your undergraduate
   program and the graduate or professional course of study that you
   anticipate; hence, it is foolish to regard a graduate program as a
   mere extension of your current work.

2. You may be tempted to choose a course of graduate study before
   you have sufficiently explored the world of work to chart a career
   direction. This kind of premature decision-making can only lead
   to uncertainties at a later date.

3. You may have a natural tendency to continue your education simply
   because it offers you the opportunity to continue in an environment
   which you find familiar and comfortable; such a path may be enjoyable in the short run, but disastrous in the long run because
   you may have invested yourself in a field that you know little about.

Often, the graduate school decision is made on the basis of a program of
course work that sounds good and holds a vague promise of interesting employment. In more cases than people are willing to admit, the graduate school applicant has only a dim awareness of the kinds of work which lie at the end of the
graduate school pipeline. This means that you may apply for a graduate program
in, say, Urban Planning, without having ever had more than a passing conversation with people who do this kind of work for a living. It is this kind of myopia
which can turn an exciting graduate school adventure into a wild goose chase that
has only incidental meaning for your personal goals in life.

Nonetheless, once you have finished the B.A. or B.S., you may feel a
strong urge to move directly into additional education. This rush to graduate
and professional schools is ordinarily justified on three counts: (1) There is
continuity between undergraduate learning and the specialized concentration of
a graduate field; (2) It is easier to finance graduate study when other obligations

such as marriage, mortgages, etc., can be delayed; and (3) It seems advisable to get all of one's educational preparation out of the way, before proceeding with one's career development.

These arguments have been bought on a wholesale basis by many of today's liberal arts graduates, and it is unfortunate that the reasoning is so frequently flawed. Many students fear that they will forget all of what they have learned, and even lose all memory of how to study once they have been away from school. This is simply not so. You may lose the motivation for academic work because of competing needs, but you will retain for a long period the principles you have learned and the general ability to perform academic tasks. Thus, the continuity argument is not so all-embracing as many would have us believe. Often, it is a fiction which attracts people who want to stay in the comfort zone of an educational institution a while longer before accepting the responsibility of a work role.

Furthermore, the argument that one must complete one's education before proceeding with a career must be a classic example of a cart which can precede the horse. Many people do not know where the educational chariot is leading them when they get aboard; they may find it a comfortable ride but they will be no more certain of their career goals when the destination is reached because the education in itself is not sufficient to expose people to the work possibilities which may come later.

Graduate and professional schools are beginning to recognize that they sometimes pay a price for enticing students to enlist in their programs directly after undergraduate school. While the young graduate student may be scholastically sound and unencumbered by family or other obligations, he often comes burdened with certain liabilities that can hinder his education progress:

1. He can be uncertain about the purpose of his graduate study, where it will lead him and why he came in the first place;

2. He may be footloose, suffering from a conflict between his educational goal and the desire to travel, have a big time in the city and meet lots of interesting people; and

3. He may be unable or unwilling to grow into a professional role without some non-academic life experience.

Many graduate and professional schools now prefer applicants who have had some relevant experience beyond their undergraduate years. Schools of journalism, law, business, social work, education, counseling, and others are notable examples. Medical schools are a prominent exception, and there are others who still prefer to take applicants directly from undergraduate school. The trend toward applicants with work experience is not a wholesale, one-sided change of attitude among admissions committees, but it is a noticeable factor in the increased difficulty that recent B.A. graduates have encountered in attempting to gain acceptance to the graduate and professional schools of their choice.

It is the author's position that, as a liberal arts graduate, you should:

1. Make a systematic review of your career objectives in a thorough program designed for this purpose before considering enrollment in a graduate or professional program;

2. Obtain practical exposure to areas of work that interest you before committing yourself to a graduate or professional program.

After the liberal arts graduate has been exposed to the work that he thinks is most suitable (either through actual jobs or extended conversations with working people), has seen how his education can be applied in real terms to problems of an employer, and has reached some agreement with himself about future career goals, then he should try to acquire whatever specialized training may be demanded by his chosen field. A rich mixture of work experience, the ability to see the whole rather than the parts, and the necessary specialized knowledge is a potent combination and can propel liberal arts graduates into positions of responsibility and challenge.

Today, many liberal arts graduates take refuge in graduate or professional schools to avoid the pain of job hunting or the uncertainty of having to make a vocational commitment. Unfortunately, the choice of a graduate program is often an unwitting but potential commitment because an advanced degree may channel you into a vocational pipeline from which it will be difficult to dislodge yourself. You might say to yourself, "If I went through all this education, I must be pretty sure of what I want to do," and then discover some years later that your decision was premature.

The years following undergraduate school can be a time for reflection, exploration, and taking a long look around at your possibilities. Jobs can be accepted chiefly for the purpose of observing and testing your perceptions of vocational realities. However, if you do not explore, the early 20's of your life can be spoiled or distorted by shaky career commitments. These years can be filled with many reality-testing experiences. There is a delicate settling process which must occur in the blending of your interests, values, and career goals. Self-reflections ordinarily should be tempered by exposure to work, before you can make any sense of your future goals.

The Liberal Arts Predicament

It is no accident of fate that liberal arts students have the most difficulty making up their minds about career possibilities. The problems of career uncertainty seem to dog the liberal arts student in every step of his educational journey.

If you are typical of many liberal arts students, you face a dilemma of plenty; there are so many different topics that interest you, it seems rather impossible to choose among them. Or, do you feel that you have learned a little about a lot of things but nothing in sufficient depth to provide a direction? This is less a dilemma than it is an embarrassment of riches. As we shall learn later, in the course of the PATH exercises, a variety of interests and knowledge can be coalesced into a far better career than single-minded concentration upon one area of knowledge.

Talking with graduates of liberal arts colleges during the past several years, I have discovered that most were able to find one kind of job or another after some searching around, but their job choices too seldom emerged from an active process of exploring the kinds of work they believe they would like best. As a result I found that two problems often would surface three to five years after these liberal arts graduates had been in the labor market, graduate school, or both:

1. They suspect that their vocational decisions were made according to the "accidental" theory; they took what was available at the time whether it was a job, an opening in graduate school, or some other handy opportunity.

2. They have fallen into a comfortable rut of making money, being "not too dissatisfied" with their jobs, and becoming afraid that the comfort and security has become a habit that is difficult to break.

Thus, we see that the richly endowed liberal arts graduate can be immobilized by his own accidental career decision process. You may fall into one job or another, acquire some experience in it, and then fear to make a change to something that you like better because the whole working world seems so "specialized" and you do not want to start all over again learning a new career.

These problems touch the roots of what basically ails the liberal arts student today. As one who was born into a world of specialized labor, advanced technology, and resident "experts," the seeker of the liberal education will face four peculiar problems in his efforts to find a satisfying place in the world of employment:

1. In a world of specialists, how do I make a case for the "generalist" approach to human affairs where a problem is not solved by expertise in a special domain but through an understanding of the whole?

2. Knowing that I have a rather diverse collection of talents and interests, how do I decide what kinds of work to pursue?

3. Without having had any exposure to real employment during my educational years, how can I match my personal needs with what a job may have to offer?

4. Most importantly, how do I choose a vocation that is compatible with my personal needs, the style in which I want to live, the way I want to relate to my environment, and the goals that I hope to accomplish?

The truth is, bluntly, that many jobs in the working world are less specialized than you think they are, and you have considerable freedom to shift around before finding an area where your unique combination of talents can best be applied. As a liberal arts graduate, you will have greater flexibility than most people because your education has led you into many areas of knowledge and, consequently, has whetted your appetite for many interesting combinations of work.

The Value of a Liberal Arts Education in the World of Work

You are a liberal arts student who is being educated to think with clarity, understand man's cultural and historical roots, deal with problems in an inter-disciplinary way, and recognize the necessity for living humanely in a product-oriented, technological world.

You are well aware of the dangers of indecision, but somehow the prospect of taking aim on a career seems too much like a life sentence. You have spent four years in the castle of higher education. Now someone is going to let down the drawbridge and you are expected to know all about the countryside and what kinds of hunting are profitable there. [1]

It is true that increasing specialization of labor will make it difficult for the liberal arts graduate to compete for employment especially when he or she is seeking the first job. However, as the liberal arts graduate acquires job experience, the disadvantages of a non-technical education are reduced and the assets of a liberal education begin to pay dividends.

Your broad education will provide that most precious of commodities in today's labor market — flexibility. And, as the numbers of specialists continue to mount, there is likely to be a counter-trend toward the liberal arts graduate, particularly if he or she accumulates broad experience in the worlds of private and public enterprise.

The value of the liberal arts degree in job markets can be expressed in several ways:

(a) The ability to communicate with clarity to a variety of audiences, in writing, orally, and in other media;

(b) The inter-disciplinary viewpoint, an ability to understand a situation from several different points of view, seeing matters in a larger perspective, and envisioning creative solutions to old problems;

(c) The capacity to understand man's technological decisions in human terms, to make decisions that enable people to live together more humanely;

(d) The recognition that most failures are breakdowns not in the productivity of a system but a deterioration of the relationships among the people who inhabit the system; and

(e) Flexibility in rapidly changing job markets; in a society where jobs sometimes turn inside-out within five to ten years, the liberal arts graduate is capable of turning a seemingly unrelated combination of talents into a viable job.

---

1. The analogy has been borrowed with permission from Ms. Judith Katz, Director of Career Planning, Swarthmore College, who discussed it in a talk entitled, "The Extern Program," delivered to the Middle Atlantic Placement Association at Westminster College, June 28, 1973.

Generalists vs. Specialists

Private and public enterprise alike have stepped up their demands for specially trained personnel, just as colleges and junior colleges in particular have expanded their numbers of specialty-oriented major fields of study. Is it better to be a specialist in the heightened competition among college graduates? In many respects, the armor of a specialty is good protection against the whims of employers and the uncertainties of future job markets, because capable specialists are sometimes hard to find.

On the other hand, in an economy where more and more college degree-holders come equipped with a specific kind of education or training, the broad-thinking, more versatile generalist (who graduates from a liberal arts program) may find that there is a premium on his talents. A diverse collection of specialists often needs a generalist to coordinate their talents and decide how their special abilities can best be used. A generalist has just enough exposure to special job areas to know what they can do, and enough breadth in his experience to see how special talents can be combined in new ways.

The Need for Experience

The lack of experience is a prominent bugaboo for all liberal arts graduates when they finish their B.A. or B.S. degrees because most organizations are reluctant to hire the untried college idealist. However, if the liberal arts graduate is alert enough to take the long view, experience can become his leading asset over a period of years. The author strongly recommends that you use your 20's to land as many different kinds of work as possible. This may mean taking several different kinds of jobs in widely varying settings (i.e., insurance, journalism, government, social service, manufacturing, etc.) before aspiring to a higher level of work.

After you have gotten around to many different corners of the working world, you will be sought for the breadth of your experience. If you have been in private industry, government, education, and non-profit work, then you know a great deal about how these sectors relate to each other. If you are conversant with both sides of the desk in a government-industry dispute, for example, you are more valuable than the person who has known only one side. When it is necessary to understand a certain kind of organization (such as a manufacturing firm, federal regulatory agency, etc.), there is no adequate substitute for having worked there at some time in your past. As private, public, and other organizations develop more and more contacts and relationships with each other, the people in demand will be those who can articulate between them.

Test Batteries

Unfortunately, most liberal arts graduates lack work experience at the time they complete their education and they often find themselves taking potluck in the world of work. To many, the prospect of randomly casting about for a job creates an uncomfortable feeling. To forestall this feeling, some will turn to aptitude tests and other measurement devices.

Many of you have already had experience with standardized tests given by high school or college counselors. Some of you have benefitted by this approach, but many others are left disillusioned because the outcomes of the test batteries disagree with your own views of your vocational possibilities.

Often the results of testing lead an individual to over-interpret their meaning. The individual hears the outcomes of his tests, ignores the counselor's cautions about the limited predictive value of such results and proceeds to plot a career direction from what he or she has learned about himself. Years later, the individual may discover that he wishes he were doing a different kind of work, but he has already invested himself in the occupation designated by the test data and is reluctant to make a significant change.

Standardized tests offer you an opportunity to measure some of your personal attributes and compare yourself with other people. Some measures, notably interest inventories, offer you the chance to classify the results in an occupational context (i.e., "How do my interests compare with those of lawyers, accountants, etc.?" on the Strong Vocational Interest Blank). However, the PATH approach prefers to by-pass the acknowledged utility of such information for these reasons:

1. It is dangerously premature to measure a person's attributes and ascribe occupational significance to the results before the person has done a thorough self-evaluation of his vocationally-related needs and objectives;

2. The author wishes to de-emphasize the individual's relative standing (compared to normative groups) in career evaluation, and emphasize instead his absolute needs and talents (what do I want to do? what are my most prominent attributes, etc.?); and

3. The results of standardized tests are subject to frequent and gross misinterpretation by the individuals who take them, despite the best interpretative efforts of counselors, testmakers and others.

In order to avoid the kind of misinterpretation and over-interpretation that occurs frequently with the use of standardized tests in career counseling, PATH has been designed to rely entirely on self-evaluation. Instead of turning to external analyses to help you make career decisions, the PATH exercises direct you to rely upon your internal assessment and translate these self-assessments into occupational significance.

Testing has been the natural outgrowth of a heavy reliance upon trait theory in vocational guidance. However, as Thorndike and Hagen discovered:

"There is no convincing evidence that aptitude tests ... can predict degree of success within an occupation insofar as this is represented in the criterion measures that we were able to obtain. This would suggest that we should view the long-range

prediction of occupational success by aptitude tests with a good
deal of skepticism and take a very restrained view as to how
much can be accomplished in this direction. " [2]

Martin R. Katz, in <u>Decisions and Values</u>, has a pointed comment about
the aptitude tests and other measures used by vocational guidance counselors:

"They try to combine putative predictors impressionistically rather
than actuarially and then attribute exaggerated validity to their judgments. Their simple-minded attempts to match pupils' occupational
and educational choices to traits in a pat way often ignore the sub-
stantive empirical data that are available. " [3]

A useful alternative to testing is to ask you to supply self-ratings of your
own attributes. Self-assessment in PATH is used to cue you about career possibilities, but it does not attempt to predict future choices. The program is not
concerned with discovering a one-to-one correspondence between the career
you say you want today and the career which ultimately will satisfy you.

It would be a mistake also to think that your self-ratings are entirely
accurate; they are always subject to self-distortion. If your judgments of yourself are distorted or inflated, you will learn this in the crucible of experience
or by investigating vocations before you decide to enter them.

Most importantly, self-ratings do not require complicated explanations
by a counselor or psychologist. Thus, whatever the outcomes of the PATH
Program, they will not be mysterious to you. The directions that you chart
will be understandable because they will be a product of your own self-evaluations.
If you arrive at a conclusion that seems doubtful or inconsistent, you are free
to revise the input that you have given in PATH and change direction.

People choose their careers with one eye closed and their fingers crossed.
They often seize upon whatever job opportunities happen to cross their path and
discover only when they are immersed in the work that it is either boring, un-
suited to their talents or distasteful in some way.

Inspired by the wit and candor of Peter Sandman's <u>Unabashed Career
Guide</u>.[4] I maintain that most of our visions of careers are the product of noble
ideals, vague perceptions of a job that somebody else is doing, or promotional
material from the offices of a professional association. If you were to believe
what you read in occupational literature, novels, or autobiographies about
people and their vocations, then <u>all</u> careers are potentially wondrous and capable of inspiring you to heights of ecstasy.

Not only does career literature and the popular press give us a semi-
fictional view of life in the operating room, the press room, or the court of law,
it also tends to keep our images of careers rooted in the past. We see what has
already happened and try to emulate the heroes of yesterday rather than set off
on new trails and new endeavors. There is a danger in following the footsteps
of others into a vocation because our elders may remember only the good times.
Furthermore, a vocation can change greatly from one generation to the next.

––––––––––

2. Robert Thorndike and Elizabeth Hagen, *Ten Thousand Careers*. New York: John Wiley & Sons, 1959.

3. Martin R. Katz, *Decisions and Values*. New York: College Entrance Examination Board, 1963, pgs. 9 and 11.

4. Peter Sandman, *The Unabashed Career Guide*. London: Collier Books, 1969, pg. 18.

Is There One Best Job For You?

Most of our career decision making is heavily oriented toward <u>convergent</u> thinking. Such an approach states that there is one best solution to your vocational needs, and your job is to identify what vocation that is. Thus, some decision-making programs engage you in identifying vocational alternatives, assigning values to the various aspects of a vocation, determining probabilities of success and arriving at a "best" choice based upon the product of desirability (value) and the probability of success. Although this may be a reasonable way to make a decision in the short run, it has the unfortunate consequence of seeming rather final. You have converged upon a single answer to your decision problem and tend to accept this conclusion without room for adjustment in the future.

What you need more than a convergent, single-decision type of program is a method that encourages and rewards <u>divergent</u> thinking, which is creative rambling, about the many ways in which your personal and vocational needs might be satisfied. Put simply, you are a person of many needs and interests, and there are probably numerous kinds of work which have the potential for making you happy.

There is a corollary to the convergent mind-set in vocational decision-making which says that once you have found your intended career you must never let it go, devote yourself to it, commit your energies to it, and drive yourself to be as productive as possible within your chosen realm. On the contrary, thinking divergently (creatively) about your vocation suggests that you should be reluctant to make a final commitment to all-out pursuit of a single career. You should be looking for a combination of work activities that you find rewarding; but they should not be so binding that you could not leave them when you feel the urge to do something different.

Do not be put off by employers (and there are many of them) who say that they have a hard time finding places for liberal arts graduates because they have no specific job skills. Employers say this because they are quite ignorant of your talents and they do not know how to rate you against a business school graduate; they simply do not know what to do with you. Consequently, you will have to educate them.

Assume that the job you would most like to do in the world does not yet exist. That's right, you are going to write your own job description, complete with job duties, advancement ladder and expected satisfactions. That is, if you are smart, you will do so. We are living in Future Shock and you can turn this phenomenon to your advantage. For every job which is rendered obsolete, there is someone who has thought of a new way to solve old needs. Wherever you can spot an unmet need, or an unsolved problem, you have found yourself a potential job. Employers forget about job qualifications very rapidly when they discover that you have something in your tool kit that can help to improve the performance of their organization.

The idea of creating your own career is not a new one. Remember the guy who built the better mousetrap? A "created" job is one where you can bring new talents and fresh ways of conceiving a problem to an old, old situation. All across the landscape, there are people who are doing their jobs badly, inefficiently, lackadaisically, or not at all. This is not because they are incompetent, useless people. It is because the people are misplaced in their positions. As Richard Irish says in Go Hire Yourself an Employer:

> "The striking characteristic of all employment relationships is there is no such thing as the wrong people: there are only people mismatched against the wrong jobs." [5]

But, you are thinking, this business of creating your own career is radical stuff. It is idealistic, the product of blue-sky dreaming and difficult to apply to your own situation. It just doesn't make sense that a person could dream up his own opportunity and then find a pasture where it can be made to come true.

Before dealing with your natural skepticism, it will be helpful to take a look at the ways in which you might ordinarily approach the process of making a career decision.

If you will look closely at the style of career decision making you have followed up to this time, you are likely to find one of the following:

1. The Divine Calling — "I have known what my life's work will be ever since the age of 10 so there is really no need to explore this question at all."

2. Hang Loose — "I am keeping my options as open as possible for as long as possible because I have no idea what life holds in store for me and I don't even want to think about it."

3. Grocery Store Mentality — "Just tell me what's available (on the grocery shelf of work opportunities) and I will choose the one that is most attractively packaged."

If you are trying to decide which of these approaches would serve you best, the answer is: None of the Above. All three have in common this basic defect: They permit other people to have control over your decision process.

If you choose according to the Divine Calling, you may believe that you made the decision yourself at a tender age, but in truth the decision probably emerged from the presence of a powerful role model (parent, uncle, etc.) or the sum of family and social pressures toward one career or another.

People who choose careers before they enter junior high school are saying that they made a choice which is central to their own identity before they even began to have an identity. They fall in the same category as people who get married after three dates, choose a college from a descriptive brochure, or buy a home from an advertisement in the newspaper.

The Hang Loose decision-maker is easy prey for the Race Track Tout method of career advising. "Come here a minute, son, I think a good bet

---

5. Richard Irish, *Go Hire Yourself an Employer*. New York: Doubleday, Anchor Press, 1973, pg. 18.

for you would be ..." The person who surrenders his or her own decision to
fate or "time will take care of me" invites other people to leap into the vacuum
and propose choices that remove the burden of decision from their shoulders.

It is one thing to be open to unforeseen possibilities, but it is quite
another to use this sense of freedom as an invitation to surrender all responsibility for taking the initiative in the shaping of your career.

While Divine Calling and Hang Loose are obviously unacceptable ways
to arrive at career decisions, the Grocery Store metaphor demands even closer
attention because it is more widely contagious and has a veneer of rationality
which makes it easier to accept. Though it might seem reasonable to choose
judiciously from what is available, there are two fatal flaws in this approach:

1. You are blissfully unaware of 80 per cent of the existing categories
   of work and thus may find yourself considering only doctor, lawyer,
   Indian chief, butcher, baker and candlestickmaker;

2. By choosing only from what is offered, you allow the job to have
   control of the decision process. In truth there is no such thing as
   the job of a lawyer, businessman, social worker or journalist.
   Ridiculous statement, you say? Of course, any job title demands
   certain technical competencies and requires a certain outcome of
   the people who perform it; however, you will bring a unique combination of talents and attributes to any job that you undertake, and
   this uniqueness will (or should) transform the job into one that is
   different from the way anyone else would do it.

Try a little experiment. Ask any five people who have the same job
title what they do during a typical work week. You will discover a startingly
different array of work activities among people who presumably have the same
job.

To extend the metaphor further, you must conceive of your career as a
home-cooked meal rather than selecting fast-preparation frozen foods from the
handiest shelves. The Grocery Store approach deludes you into thinking that
only certain items are "available" when, in truth, natural ingredients can be
combined to produce a truly original end product. The secret is in the seasoning, and the seasoning in this case is your talents, needs, values and other
unique characteristics which can make your life's work different from anyone
else's.

Like any savory home-cooked meal, the trick in being able to create a
career of your own is to have sufficient time to do the job right from start to
finish. The making and baking of a career, if it is delayed until there is little
time remaining, will be no better than a frozen food facsimile of the real thing.

The preparation of a career requires time and attention. If the process
is begun early enough — several years before you are required to earn a living
— it is possible to test your perception of yourself against realities without
making any commitments or closing out other possibilities. The subtle blend of
your talents and needs is one which requires continual reshaping during childhood, adolescence and the early adult years.

One thing must be recognized about career planning the home-cooked way — it is hard work. In this light, it is easy to understand why many people settle for the advice of others, take whatever looks best on the Grocery Shelf, or retreat into indecision. The temptation of a job offered by a friend of the family, a classified ad, or a campus recruiter becomes ever more inviting as time grows short and you drift into pre-graduation panic.

However, let us not frighten you into thinking that career planning will require half of your waking hours. It will require effort, but much of the battle is knowing the right questions to ask. The PATH Program attempts to provide a structure in which to ask yourself these right questions, and a context in which to evaluate the answers. If you pay sufficient attention to these questions and avoid the premature commitments offered by friendly advice-givers, you can prepare a career that is uniquely your own rather than grabbing something hurriedly from the help-wanted columns the day before graduation.

Alternative Vocations

Most of your parents have made successes of themselves in the world of work, but is this the kind of success you want? You know all about the routes to medical school, law school, private enterprise, the scholarly life, or a career in government. Generally you can chart a course for any of these professions by obtaining the appropriate advanced degree, and then following in the steps of others who have preceded you.

But, suppose you don't want to trudge along in someone else's footsteps? Suppose you really don't care for medicine, law, selling insurance, or teaching English? Where are the jobs of tomorrow, the ones which may not have been defined yet? You suspect that there are needs in the world that have not been met but how does a person with only a B.A. or B.S. degree go about finding such jobs?

Alternative careers — jobs that do not fit the usual channels of employment or have not been around long enough to be considered traditional — are ordinarily thought of as grass-roots community work, helping roles in rural areas where most people won't go, or trying to sell hand-made products that do not have a large market. On the contrary, an alternative career can be anything you want it to be. A middle management job in a large corporation can be an alternative vocation if you think it is possible to do it differently than the ways others have done it before you. A lawyer who brings his knowledge to citizens' groups and organizes them to pursue legal grievances is practicing his profession in an alternative way.

You can define an alternative vocation as one which has some effect upon the institutions which govern our lives. Try to imagine the ways in which many traditional jobs can be practiced in an alternative way. Policemen, city managers, lawyers, artists, newspaper reporters, and sanitation men all may hold traditional jobs, but it is possible to conceive of ways that these jobs might be done differently so they could enable people to live more humanely and perhaps even have an effect upon social change.

Creative Vocations

Perhaps your thorniest problem as a liberal arts student is that there are so many different things that you would like to do. How do you make the painful choice of opting for one kind of work and discarding several others? You don't. Vocational decision-making is not an either-or proposition. The PATH workbook encourages you to practice what we call creative vocation-hunting, and assume that it is quite possible to satisfy several of your vocational needs if you look for the right kind of situation.

What does creative vocation-hunting really mean? And, how can you practice it within the boundaries of existing jobs and your limitations of talent or work experience? In all likelihood, your first two or three jobs will not be creative at all but will be chosen on the basis of expediency. However, it is not these early choices themselves which matter, but the way in which they can build toward more creative opportunities in the future. In order to chart a path which will help you to make your ideal job become real, you must:

1. Engage yourself in the process of identifying all the desirable elements that you'd like to have in a single kind of work.

2. Use each successive job to prepare yourself for a better one by acquiring experience which has value and knowledge that can be useful to a future employer.

3. Concentrate upon finding problems to be solved, rather than looking for existing jobs; show an employer how you can deal with old problems in a new way.

This latter stage is the ultimate in creative vocation-hunting, because it involves you in defining a job description that best suits your talents, experiences, and work preferences. It is within your power to reach for jobs that do not yet exist.

In times of rapid change, social tensions, and rampant obsolescence in occupational fields, it is more true than ever that the man (or woman) can make the job rather than the reverse idiom. Jobs are not pigeonholes. There is little reason for the educated man to think he must adhere to a job description that may have been written 10 or 20 years ago.

Of many jobs and the way they are performed, it might be said, "In the land of the blind, the one-eyed man is king." Liberal arts graduates often come to new jobs with two eyes open and do not realize their potential. Although the lessons of past experience are valuable and have much to teach the neophyte, there is always room for a new vision, a new way of looking at a job, and a creative solution to an old problem.

Summary

As you begin the PATH Program, you will discover that it differs fundamentally from many traditional methods of vocational guidance in several ways. Each of the general principles described below is a concept that you must read and assimilate before you initiate the program.

(1) <u>Your Career Decisions Reflect Who You Are As A Whole Person</u>

It is not possible or even desirable to separate your vocational self from the rest of your being. Since the work you do should reflect some of your strongest needs, it should be an accurate reflection of you as a total person.

(2) <u>Your College Major May Not Be Related To Your Career Objective</u>

There is no necessary or required linkage between your major field of study and the career(s) you may eventually pursue.

(3) <u>Do Not Use Graduate School As A Refuge From Career Decision-Making</u>

Do not enroll in a graduate or professional school unless you have developed a career objective that you are reasonably confident will satisfy your primary vocational needs.

(4) <u>You Are The Best Judge Of Yourself</u>

All judgments about your suitability for various kinds of work, the strengths that you do or do not possess, the careers that you want to know more about, etc., will be made by you. You know yourself best and you should be at the center of any career decision process.

(5) <u>Fantasy Is Good For You</u>

Fantasy is perhaps the most effective stimulus to the development of a career that will elicit your maximum effort. It is crucial that you have a vision of what you would most like to accomplish in life, because this vision will shape the kinds of opportunities you seek to create for yourself.

(6) <u>Job Labels Are Arbitrary</u>

A job description should never be accepted at face value. You should attempt to reshape a job to suit your special needs and talents. In many situations, you can perform new functions under an old job label.

(7) <u>Create Your Own Career</u>

It is very likely that, over a period of years, you can approach an ideal career by blending parts of existing occupations into a creative and new kind of work. It is necessary to think divergently (there are many different things that I can do) rather than convergently (there is only one best job for me) in order to develop a creative career.

(8) <u>Value Your Liberal Education</u>

Your liberal education provides you conceptual breadth and vision
that cannot be claimed by a graduate from a specialized educational
program. A similar value can be derived from work experience,
in that a diversity of jobs creates its own special value that cannot
be claimed by the specialist who has done one kind of work for a
long period of time.

(9) <u>Recognize That Your Needs Can Change</u>

Whatever decisions you may make, be alert to the subtle shifts in
your vocational needs which may occur. Ideally, the career commitment that you make should be a renewable contract with yourself, subject to review every two to five years.

(10) <u>Know That Nothing In Your Career Will Be Wasted</u>

Regardless of the shifts that you may make between your jobs or from
one career to another, the experiences that you acquire will have a
cumulative effect upon every job you take. You will be able to apply
what you have learned in one job when you change to another.

Section II:

PREMISES of the PATH PROGRAM

The PATH Program assumes that you have the following capabilities:

1. You are capable of making your own vocational decisions.

2. You are able to make use of your strongest attributes in the world of work.

3. You can act upon your environment in order to create changes in your career when your work experience convinces you that a change is necessary.

4. You are capable of doing many different kinds of work.

> "Occupations require a characteristic pattern of abilities, interests, and personality traits, with tolerances wide enough, however, to allow both some variety of occupations for each individual and some variety of individuals in each occupation." [6]

Thus, it is clear that when you seek guidance in your career process, you are asking not only that you receive assistance with an immediate decision, but also that you learn principles of career development which can be used for an extended period of time. Since you have the potential to qualify for several different vocations in your lifetime and the vocational environment changes often enough so that you will probably make use of your "multipotentiality," it is necessary that any vocational guidance program take this long view.

Individuality and Freedom in the Career Process

Ideally, a vocation can be a coherent expression of what you want from your life. The possibilities for satisfaction in a vocation are numerous, but you must have an appreciation for the subtle nature of the process by which individuals decide the kinds of work they are going to do.

---

6. Donald E. Super, "A Theory of Vocational Development." *American Psychologist*, 1953. pgs. 185-190.

The vocational decision is a highly subjective process, one in which the delicate interactions between factors are understood perhaps only by the person who is weighing them. Exercises such as these in the PATH Program can contribute information to the whole but they cannot be directly interpreted for final answers. The subtle blend of influences, which constitute a vocational decision, will probably change its colors many times. We can live with this process, as long as we are reasonably in control of it, and aware of changes in our needs as they take place.

It is perhaps fair to say that vocational choice will resist the attempts of some scientists to analyze it as a process having predictable outcomes. Since vocational needs are forever intertwined with all the complex motivations of an individual, we cannot expect to reduce a vocational decision to predictable, orderly terms. Nor do we want to do so.

> "Uncertainty is not only the plainest condition of human life
> but the necessary condition of freedom, of aspiration, of
> conscience, of all human idealism. ... Pretensions to ab-
> solute certainty ... are the ultimate source of corruption,
> the reasons why the best become the worst, and crusaders
> for heaven make a hell on earth." [7]

Limitations of Freedom and Individual Incentive

It is well to offer a few sobering thoughts about the freedom of individual choice and the value of individualism which are so clearly represented by the nature of this program.

1. It is difficult today to erect a castle of your individual vocational goals and achieve these goals on your own. As long ago as 1911, Frederick Winslow Taylor noted —

   "The time is fast going by for the great personal or individual achievement of any one man, standing alone and without the help of those around him. In the past, man has been first; in the future, the systems must be first." [8]

2. The increased tendency toward providing "something for everyone" — a movement toward equal sharing of economic rewards, participation in work tasks (e.g., decision by committee, participatory democracy) will make individual goals harder to achieve.

3. In a very real sense, these trends signal the weakening of the tradition of individualism. While PATH is rooted in this tradition, it seems reasonable to modify the individual-can-go-it-alone viewpoint and declare that individual goals can often be pursued cooperatively and within the context of societal goals.

---

7. Herbert J. Muller, *Uses of the Past*. New York: Oxford University Press, 1953. pg. 43.

8. F. W. Taylor, "On the Art of Cutting Metals" in *Transactions of the American Society of Mechanical Engineers*, 1907, Volume 28, pg. 57.

4. Aaron Levenstein suggests that the decline of individual rewards inherent in technological society must be supplanted by rewards that emphasize one's contribution to society through one's work role —

"Within the community, the individual plays an important role because of the very complexity and interdependence resulting from increased numbers and from the technology of affluence that has accompanied size. Now all can suffer at the hands of one. The mind stumbles in the presence of the awful fact that one individual in a plane can push the button that will release the nuclear holocaust. One man in an automated oil refinery, by malice or by simple neglect, can bring the whole process to a halt." [9]

Long before this interdependence had become as prevalent as it is today, William James wrote:

"A social organism is what it is because each member proceeds to his own duty with a trust that other members will simultaneously do theirs. A government, an army, a commercial system, a ship, a college, an athletic team, all exist on this condition without which not only is nothing achieved, but nothing is even attempted." [10]

Job Labels Are Arbitrary

As you read about occupations and jobs, and then investigate them in actual job settings, you will soon discover that there are great differences between what the popular literature tells you and what a given individual may actually be doing in a vocation. This is understandably true for two reasons:

1. Different people can do the same job in a variety of different ways. The higher the level of occupational responsibility, the more an individual's peculiar style of operating can affect the way in which the work gets done. Differences in work style are found among accountants, newspaper reporters, counselors, businessmen and almost any occupation.

2. The job that a person does, especially at higher levels of responsibility, is almost never the same job that appears in the job description. It is usually a hybrid of the formal job requirements and some other set of job duties that the individual has incorporated into his work.

The somewhat arbitrary and fluid nature of job titles should not discourage you. You can use general labels for occupations as a first step toward a survey of the kinds of work which are available to you. Once you have determined your preferences among fields that are widely different, you should begin

9. Aaron Levenstein, "Work and Its Meaning in an Age of Affluence," in *Career Guidance for a New Age* edited by Henry Borow. Boston: Houghton-Mifflin Co., 1973, pg. 146.

10. Stuart Chase, *The Proper Study of Mankind*. New York: Harper, 1948, pg. 62.

the more direct investigation which will tell you subtle differences among jobs that appear to be similar.

Acting on Partial Information

It is an axiom of this program that all vocational decisions are made on the basis of incomplete information about (a) self and (b) the external world. Because we recognize the continual presence of uncertainty in the vocational choices that we make, it is necessary to state several conditions to the individual who completes the PATH Program.

1. Although you may use the PATH Program to integrate your vocational possibilities into what seems a congenial and satisfying career, you are liable to change this view of the "ideal" vocation at any time, based upon new information and experience you acquire.

2. A change of direction can be as small as a shift to a different employer in the same vocational field and as large as a complete reversal of preference from one vocation to another that is entirely different.

3. When you feel that your vocational needs have changed, you may review any vocation that you may have rejected in the past because your new information and experience may dictate a new disposition about this vocation.

4. In your efforts to close the gap of missing information about your vocational alternatives, rely as much as possible upon personal investigation and actual work experience.

No matter how certain you may feel about your career decision, it pays to cultivate a certain amount of doubt so that your mind will remain open to other possibilities.

Why PATH Ignores Job Market Supply and Demand

When confronted with having to make a career decision, many students ask:

"What are the best fields to get into?"

"Where are the most job opportunities?"

You may believe that certain vocational fields should be avoided if they show a declining volume of job opportunities, regardless of how strong your inclination toward such fields may be. Nonetheless, PATH attempts to minimize supply and demand orientation as much as possible, as a factor in career decision-making, for the following reasons:

1. Supply and demand data bear little relationship to your needs, values and life priorities. Since the latter are regarded as primary in this program, acceptance of the former as a potent factor in career development would undermine your internal motivation.

2. The supply and demand for people in various occupations changes rapidly and can be often dramatically different (for a given occupation) between the time that you enter college and the time you may decide to make a career commitment.

3. Even in situations where you may desire a career that is experiencing low demand, you can obtain a place in this field through sufficient effort, geographical flexibility, persistence in finding where the opportunities are, and the acquisition of appropriate vocational skills and experience.

4. Focus upon supply and demand tends to introduce a passive element to the career decision process. It assumes there is no ability on your part to act upon your environment and create new job opportunities where previously there have been none. This program prefers to emphasize your ability to generate new demand for a vocation, if your desire and talent for this kind of work are strong enough.

Is Major Related to Vocation for the Liberal Arts Graduate?

It is a prevailing myth that your choice of a major field is intimately linked to the work you will do in the future. While this connection is certainly true for some liberal arts graduates, major and vocation are very much unrelated for many others. Many parents send their children to college to learn something "practical" that will get them a job someday. However, both you and your family should recognize that the value of a liberal education cannot be interpreted so rigidly that is is seen as preparation for a vocational field.

There is not enough room in the world for all the biology majors to become biologists, all the history majors to become historians, and so forth. Although the college is mapped along departmental lines, there is no reason to believe that the world of work is organized in this way. Hence, many liberal arts graduates must, by necessity, explore vocations that have little or no direct correspondence to their major fields.

Of course it is true that large numbers of jobs depend upon educational programs to supply new manpower, but most of such programs exist in colleges other than liberal arts institutions. More importantly, for you, there are numerous jobs which do not depend upon educational programs to fill vacancies and train new leaders. The plain truth is that many, many jobs are learned through experience rather than prior education.

Your liberal education is built upon the principle that everyone who comes to your college should study many of the same disciplines and be exposed to certain common understandings of the human condition. Communality is built into the curriculum and, to the extent that a required core of courses exist, the college is resisting the notion that students should plan their coursework toward different vocational goals. Even when you undertake a major concentration, the offerings are somewhat limited so that you cannot build an entire training program for a vocation.

Many of you would point out that large numbers of liberal arts students use their undergraduate learning as a springboard for entry into various master's and doctoral programs. Of course, there is plenty of evidence of this, but it does not mean that the undergraduate student must major in a particular field in order to aspire to a particular profession. In many scholarly disciplines, only five or six courses are required for entry into graduate school, provided that the student has shown sufficient potential in other ways. Furthermore, in situations where the graduate school applicant lacks certain prerequisites, he can acquire these after receiving his B. A. degree.

Is PATH Too "Vocationally Oriented"?

If you are a faculty member, you may protest as you read PATH that it will push students down the anti-educational road of entrapment; namely, that it will make the student think of his education as preparation for a "vocation."

On the contrary, I believe that PATH will succeed in liberating students from what I call the "vocational reflex," a reaction born of insecurity which leads many students to link their education with a vocation ("I'll major in psychology so that I can get a job in social service").

Most students succumb to the "vocational reflex" because they know so little about themselves; each feels that he or she must fill this vacuum with a premature vocational choice.

The PATH Program is designed to give a student enough insight into himself and his career possibilities, and teach him enough about the most effective process for developing career directions that he will not feel compelled to make premature choices. If PATH works properly, the student will be secure in the knowledge that: (a) There are several different kinds of work that he can enjoy and do well; (b) His educational choices (e. g., choice of major) do not necessarily have to be linked to his vocational directions; (c) There is sufficient flexibility in the world of work that he will be able to find (or create) situations where his unique combination of talents and values will be welcome.

Thus, by liberating the student from the impulse to choose a career "before it's too late," PATH will encourage the student to feel more freedom within his academic program. Even more importantly, it will enable the student to see how his academic program and his future vocational goals can be integrated in ways that will reinforce each other.

<u>Summary</u>

It should be noted that the PATH Program makes certain assumptions about the process of career decision-making, and thus requires the participant to behave toward the career process in particular ways. The following premises are implicit in the exercises of the PATH Program:

(1) <u>Psychological-Internal</u>

Most of the exercises in PATH focus upon the internal, psychological dimensions of career development, the forces within you which influence you to make certain choices. Sociological and economic determinants of career development are given less emphasis.

(2) <u>Developmental</u>

Career is treated primarily as a process that involves many choice points and extends over a lifetime, rather than as a static, one-time decision.

(3) <u>Conscious</u>

It is assumed that you can bring most of your psychological-internal determinants of career development into consciousness, and that you will not be markedly affected by unconscious needs or drives.

(4) <u>Systematic</u>

The total program attempts to create a systematic procedure for examining your career development, one that takes you through an orderly sequence of exercises and eliminates, as much as possible, chance or random variation in your decision-making.

(5) <u>Multipotential</u>

You are considered capable of gaining success and satisfaction in a wide variety of vocational settings.

(6) <u>Self-Evaluative</u>

Any judgments about your relative or absolute capability for certain vocational tasks or roles are generated by you yourself (internally) rather than by making use of empirical data and externally generated evaluations.

(7) <u>Integrative</u>

Vocational decisions are assumed to be closely related, not separated from, other key decisions in your life; the total set of your value priorities is considered relevant.

(8) <u>Incomplete Information</u>

It is recognized that any given decision in a career process is based upon partial information, and this element of uncertainty makes it likely that you will alter your career process in the future, as you learn from additional vocational experience.

(9) <u>Primacy of Work</u>

It is assumed that large numbers of people will continue to regard vocation as one of the key opportunities available for producing satisfaction in one's life. As Eric Hoffer says —

> "That free men should be willing to work day after day, even after their vital needs are satisfied, and that work should be seen as a mark of uprightness and manly worth, is not only unparalleled in history but remains more or less incomprehensible to many people outside the Occident." [11]

(10) <u>Cumulative</u>

Career development is a cumulative process. Rather than characterize career development as a series of choices, it is more appropriate to see the career of an individual as the progressive stockpiling of a variety of competencies, interests and experiences.

---

11. Eric Hoffer, *Ordeal of Change*. New York: Harper & Row, 1963, p. 28.

Section III:

GUIDELINES for USING the PATH PROGRAM

General Guidelines for Students using PATH on an individual basis:

1. Allow at least two or three days to elapse from one exercise to the next so that you will have enough time for personal reflection and so that you will take sufficient time to write complete responses to the questions. It is probably wise to read the questions in the next exercise a day or two before you attempt to write your responses.

2. In identifying your Abilities and Values in the various exercises, be as specific as possible.

> Example: It doesn't help much to say, "I liked English because it was exciting or intellectual." Instead, you might say, "I liked English because I could practice expository writing and I could study the styles of modern poets."

> Example: It is insufficient to say, "I did well in debate because I speak well." Instead, you might say, "I did well in debate because I have careful methods for organizing research data, I can summarize information effectively in oral presentation, and I respond well to impromptu inquiries."

3. Feel free to repeat an exercise at any time if you think that you have uncovered new information about yourself, your interpretations of your attributes have changed, or your work-related needs have undergone some changes in intensity or direction.

4. Write your responses to all questions in the exercises. Do not attempt to answer the questions in your head because such responses will be cursory and difficult to recall.

5. When responding to a question, write all of the details which occur to you. Be as specific as possible about things that you have done and things you would like to do, etc.

6. Allow between a half and a full hour for each exercise, if possible. In some of the exercises it will take this much time simply to write the responses, and you will have to allow additional time for prior reflection.

7. For any exercise, especially those where you are uncertain about your responses (i.e., you don't know if your response makes sense, you're not sure how to rate yourself, etc.), it helps to try explaining your response to another person.

8. If you really get stuck on a particular exercise, you should either skip it temporarily and go on to another one, or put away the whole PATH Program for at least a week and forget it until you feel you are ready to explore again.

9. When you are completing an exercise, or are doing the self-reflection which is vital preparation for an exercise, do not allow any distractions. You will need your fullest concentration to get enough in touch with yourself to give useful responses to all of the questions.

Guidelines for Counselors using the PATH program:

1. Most students will not have the patience to go through this program on their own, or, if they do, there are parts where they won't know what they're doing. To the uninitiated, the program may look like a Rube Goldberg machine looking for its inventor; therefore —

2. Your best bet is to use PATH as a group program. (See page 39 ff.)

3. You should regard this kind of program as an educational vehicle, one which teaches a student how to develop vocational direction. In this respect, you should work toward making this kind of a program part of your students' liberal arts curriculum.

4. Ideally, a PATH-type program could be a common learning experience for all students at a given stage in their educational-vocational development (e.g., just before deciding a major field of study). Teaching the process of career development as a common experience would enhance its value, because the students would learn from each other in the process.

5. If all of this sounds too "blue sky" or idealistic to you, consider the alternative, which is keeping your PATH-type program as a self-referral vehicle, completely apart from the curriculum. On this basis, which is where most counseling programs have to operate right now, students will take advantage of the program "when they can find time for it." On this basis, there is a severe limit to the number of students who can be reached; thus —

6. You must entice other people on your campus (e.g., faculty, student leaders) to support and share in the process of teaching career development.

7. Your best bet in trying to attract anyone to teach the program is to first let him experience the program so that it may have an impact upon his life; then you should provide appropriate training for those who want to share in the teaching process.

8. Generally, the earlier you can reach a student in his educational life at the college, the better, provided that the student is developmentally "ready" for such a program and willing to participate in it, because: (a) A student is more open to future possibilities, and there is less chance that he or she has made a premature vocational commitment; (b) He or she has more time to investigate career possibilities during college after completing the PATH program.

9. You should experiment with various sequences of the PATH Program exercises, though I recommend that you preserve the essential flow which is inherent in the "core program" (see page 41); (a) Specifying one's Values; (b) Specifying one's Abilities; (c) Creating a unique career from the total fabric represented by one's Values and Abilities.

PATH AS A GROUP WORKSHOP

Facilitated by Counselors, Faculty Members or Others

After three years of seeing students use the PATH Program in a variety of ways (by themselves, in small groups, in one-to-one counseling), I am convinced that, for most students, the program has its best effect when it is conducted in a group setting under the direction of an appropriately trained counselor or faculty member.

The group experience adds a dimension to PATH that the student cannot experience by himself. It gives the student a chance to test his self-perceptions on other people, learn something about how other people judge their capabilities and values, and engage in a beneficial process of give-and-take which sharpens a student's definition of the kinds of work he or she ought to look into. Many students have been surprised to find that, after completing PATH exercises on their own and then repeating these exercises in a group setting, they change their self-perceptions in the group and perhaps arrive at different vocational directions.

Using PATH in a Group Setting:

If you are a counselor, faculty member, or other person reading this book, and you want to use this program in a group setting with some of your students, there are several guidelines you should follow:

1. General "focus" rules

   (a) When one person talks (Focus Person), he or she must have the complete attention of all group members.

   (b) No participant is obligated to respond at any time. He or she can choose to "pass" without comment whenever desired.

   (c) The leader-facilitator should participate in all exercises, both in terms of writing responses and sharing responses with other group members.

2. All members of the group should follow all of the General Guidelines given on pages 37 and 38.

3. Group Exercises: Note that several of the PATH exercises have been specifically tagged as "Group Exercises" (Exercises 6, 9, 10, 11, 16 and 18). In any group program all of these exercises must be conducted so that the members of the group share self-assessments with each other.

4. Core of PATH Program: In conducting a small group workshop, you may decide that it is not possible to complete all 20 of the PATH exercises due to limits on the available time of the students. In this case, and this will frequently happen, you should use the "core program" of PATH exercises which is described on page 41.

5. Co-Leader: If at all possible, you should have a co-leader who is present at all group sessions; the co-leader helps you to explain the exercises, presents a clarifying point of view when the students don't understand what you are saying, and generally provides support to you as chief facilitator.

6. Flexibility: When working within the "core program," you may use any of the ten exercises for sharing among members of the group if you feel that it is desirable.

7. Timing: No session should last more than two and a half hours, uninterrupted.

8. Size of Sub-Group: When using an exercise for discussion and sharing among members of a group, always break a larger group into sub-groups of four people each. (If the numbers are not even, you may use a group of three.) Any larger number than four makes it difficult for each student to feel that he or she is participating actively.

9. Assignments: Assign as much as possible of the "alone" work between group sessions so that the group meetings can be devoted entirely to interaction among members of the sub-group of four. By "alone" work, I mean answering questions to the exercises on paper when the student is thinking and reflecting within his or her own head.

10. Entire Group: You can lead several sub-groups of four at the same time (as many as 20-24 students simultaneously), if you are sufficiently trained and circulate effectively among these sub-groups.

11. Continuity: A sub-group of four should ordinarily remain intact throughout the PATH exercises, because each member will accumulate greater knowledge of the other three as the exercises progress; thus each member will be a better helper as the program continues. You may want to make exceptions to this guideline (that is, you may want to shake up the memberships of the sub-groups), if you find that disharmony is developing in one or more of the sub-groups.

12. Active Questioning: For each exercise that involves interaction and sharing among the members, you will want to encourage active questioning and even outright challenging of viewpoints. Ordinarily, a student will learn most about himself/herself when the other three people actively probe his/her Values and Abilities and ask penetrating questions which force the student to think more clearly about what he or she has said.

13. Individual Counseling: Whenever possible, you should supplement the PATH Program in a group setting with individual counseling. Each participant should have an opportunity to meet with a counselor or faculty member at least once, following the completion of the program, in order to sharpen the results of his or her program, clarifying how he/she feels about these results and decide upon future actions.

THE "CORE PROGRAM" OF PATH

If you are going to offer the PATH Program to students in a group setting, I recommend that you use the following exercises as the nucleus of the program, and build other PATH exercises around them as time may permit. You should insist that each participant contract with you to complete this "Core Program" — otherwise, he/she will not obtain the cumulative benefit of what the program has to offer.

You will find that exercises outside of the "Core Program" can be used in other ways (as supplements to core exercises, when a student needs to clarify something; as stimulus material for one-to-one counseling; as extra assignments for students who want to explore themselves further).

Exercise #3	Attitudes Toward Work
Exercise #6	Enjoyable Activities* (including "I Want to Work With People")
Exercise #9	Work Values* ("Things I'd Like to Change" is the more appropriate part for discussion among members of the sub-group in this exercise.)
Exercise #10	Unique Experiences*
Exercise #11	Achievements*
Exercise #14	Self-Evaluation of Abilities
Exercise #15	Trial Occupations — Selection
Exercise #16	Trial Occupations — Comparison*
Exercise #17	Creating My Own Career Based Upon Values
Exercise #18	Creating My Own Career Based Upon Abilities*

* These exercises must be conducted in a format that includes sharing and active questioning among members of a sub-group of four.

Special Notes on the Use of PATH by Faculty Members

I have designed this program in the hope that faculty members at liberal arts colleges will want to embrace its principles and learn to use it in group settings with their students. As I have mentioned elsewhere in this book, I regard PATH as essentially a learning experience, as units of material which can be taught to students so that they will retain a knowledge of how to make work-related decisions on their own and develop a greater sensitivity to the need for self-exploration.

I am confident that a faculty member can learn to facilitate the PATH Program, if he or she supports its fundamental principles and has the time available to offer the program in its entirety (at least the "Core Program"). A liberal arts college will probably want to involve faculty with the PATH Program in the following way:

(1) Offer the program to a large group of interested faculty and, once the program is completed, choose a small number of these faculty who are most supportive and interested in using the program with their students.

(2) Provide necessary short-term training to these faculty members:
    (a) Experience in leading PATH groups
    (b) Sensitivity to the principles of group process
    (c) Direction in the best methods for facilitating PATH exercises

(3) Allow these faculty members to conduct the PATH Program with groups of students who have expressed a need for this kind of learning experience.

(4) Make sure that the faculty member has sufficient control over each group that he/she can involve the student in the full sequence of PATH assignments and group meetings.

If a college involves faculty members in PATH as described above, I believe it will derive the maximum benefit from the program, because: (a) Students will perceive that PATH is part of their education and not a program that is peripheral to the academic process; (b) Many faculty members have natural skills in counseling and group leadership and can apply these talents to PATH; and (c) Faculty members have on-going relationships with their students and thus may be more effective in helping the student to discover what the program means, where he or she wants to go after college, and other self-insights.

Currently there are several liberal arts colleges which are actively exploring the possibility of using some of their faculty members as facilitators of programs such as PATH, so that they may teach their students the process of charting effective career directions. Early innovators in this approach have been Berea College, Bethany College and Allegheny College.

Faculty members harboring any doubts about the PATH Program are urged to read (or re-read) "Is PATH Too Vocationally Oriented?" at the end of Section II, page 34.

Section IV:

THE EXERCISES

Exercise 1: PATHLINE

Part One: *Pathline*

On the accompanying chart, plot your development as a person to date. Be as creative as you can in entering items as reference points on the chart, starting at the lower left corner with the date of your birth; or you may want to start with some of your ancestors to show how their lives influenced the direction of yours even before you were born!

Select one direction on the chart to show time and the other to show events which have affected your life and will affect it in the future; such as, moving from one geographical area to another, changes in schooling, friends, births and deaths in the immediate family, parents' occupations, early efforts to earn money, etc.

Be sure to indicate major events in your life which were turning points where decisions were made by you or others and how they changed the direction of your life.

Star the high points in your life to date and put a big fat zero on the low points.

Then you may want to continue your solid pathline on the chart with a dotted or broken line to show the direction you expect to go in the future, covering such potential activities as — graduate school or professional school; vocational training (other than graduate or professional school); travel; military service; volunteer service; on-the-job training; entry-level or beginning jobs.

Key to Chart: (There are 70 large squares. 100 small squares in each.)
        A Star (*)   =   High point in my life
        A Zero (o)   =   Low point in my life
        A Cross (x)   =   Major turning point in my life

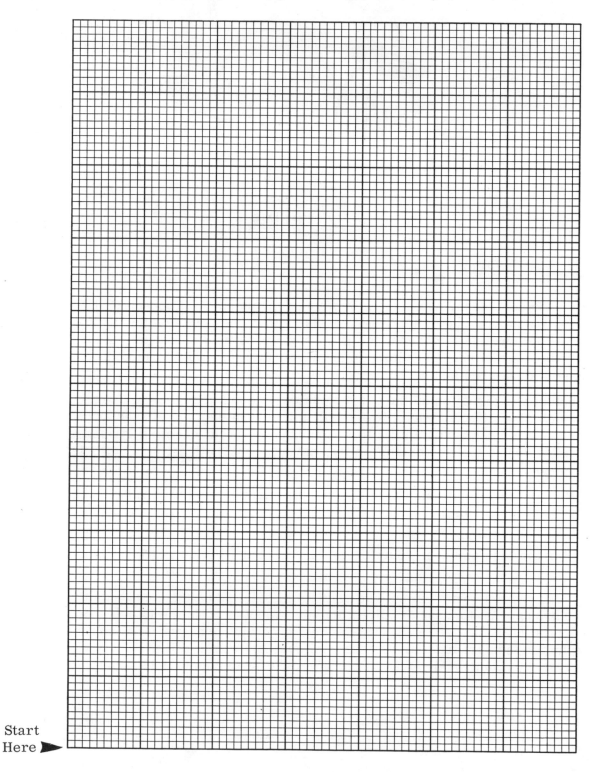

Start
Here ▶

Part Two: *Autobiography*

Imagine that you are 60 years old and are sitting down to write a brief account of the major events in your life as you recall them. Beginning at age 21, make a topical outline of the highlights or critical junctures that might occur to you if your life follows the pattern you have depicted on the chart.

Do not focus only on employment-related events. Mention all of the things that you hope will be significant to you whether or not they are events of public notice. You may write in paragraph form rather than an outline if it is easier for you. Here are some suggestions for inclusion in your autobiography:

> Significant ways in which I matured
> Prominent milestones in my life
> Major disappointments
> Turning points
> My life goals stabilized when . . .

Part Three: *One Year to Live*

Let's imagine that you've received the disheartening news that you have only one full year remaining in your life. But, you have a great deal of freedom to spend this year in the ways that suit you best.

Assume that your college education is complete — including graduate school — and you have no particular obligations to anyone unless you so choose. Thus you are free to investigate any number of possible ways to spend your year.

Within the time span of one year, select as many different activities as you wish. List at least three activities which you would give top priority to in your year and write a brief reason for its importance to you in the spaces below.

(1) ....

....

....

....

(2) ....

....

....

....

(3) ....

....

....

....

(4) ....

....

....

....

Exercise 2: CAREER FANTASIES

Part One: *Career Fantasies*

(1)   What was your most prominent career fantasy during your childhood years? Refer back to any age from four to sixteen. Tell about several fantasies, if you prefer.

....

....

....

....

(2)   What do you think of these childhood fantasies now? To what extent are they still represented in your career aspirations?

....

....

....

....

(3)   What sort of fantasies do you have today? If you could do whatever you choose, what would you do? Be as specific as possible. Describe more than one career fantasy, if you wish.

....

....

....

....

....

....

Part Two: *Ideal Vocation*

Give a brief, one paragraph composite description of all the things you would like to include in a vocation, if you had complete freedom to do so. Do not limit yourself to any one occupational label or any single kind of work activity.

(Example: I would like to work with community leaders in their efforts to help underprivileged children; write essays about the problems of the ghetto; lead an active outdoor life in the mountains; and continue to practice my creative photography.)

....

....

....

....

....

....

....

....

....

....

....

Exercise 3: ATTITUDES TOWARD WORK

Part One: *Attitudes Toward Work*

(1)   How do you feel about the whole idea of work? Check the area on the following scale which most closely represents your feelings.

Hate Work   Like Work

/	/	/	/	/	/	/	/	/	/	/	/
1	2	3	4	5	6	7	8	9	10	11	12

(2)   How important will your work be compared to your present or future family concerns? Place yourself on the scale below.

Family All-Important   Work All-Important

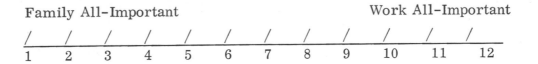

/	/	/	/	/	/	/	/	/	/	/	/
1	2	3	4	5	6	7	8	9	10	11	12

(3)   If and when you go to work, will your primary objectives be <u>intrinsic</u> (i.e. self-fulfillment, use of your abilities, personal satisfaction, etc.) or will you be seeking <u>extrinsic</u> objectives (i.e., external rewards such as money, security, power, recognition)?

Intrinsic   Extrinsic

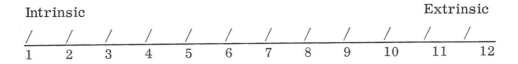

/	/	/	/	/	/	/	/	/	/	/	/
1	2	3	4	5	6	7	8	9	10	11	12

(4)   Would you work if you didn't have to? (   ) Yes   (   ) No
Explain below.

....

....

....

....

(5)   Do you expect to be fulfilled by your career? (   ) Yes   (   ) No
Explain below.

....

....

....

....

(6)   Do you make a distinction between work and leisure? Explain below.

....

....

....

(7)   If you were to decide not to work (that is, if you had the choice to
make and did not have to work for a living), how would you spend
your time?

....

....

....

....

....

....

....

....

(8)   What are your chief life priorities outside of work?

(a) ....

(b) ....

(c) ....

(d) ....

(e) ....

(f) ....

Part Two: *Things to Avoid*

If you had full freedom of choice for your ultimate vocation, what kinds of responsibilities and duties would you definitely prefer <u>not</u> to have to do? Think of tasks of all kinds that you personally regard as unpleasant which are often required of people in certain kinds of jobs. It doesn't matter if these tasks are desirable or undesirable by the standards of other people. It only matters how <u>you</u> personally feel about such tasks.

> (Example: I do not like to work with mathematical computations or do any work that requires numerical precision. I do not like to make speeches to large groups or act as a public representative for an organization. I do not like a job that requires a lot of travel and having to spend a high percentage of my time in motels and hotels.)

List all of the things you hope to avoid in the following spaces.

....

....

....

....

....

....

....

....

Exercise 4: HIGH SCHOOL EDUCATION

(1)   What did you like best about your high school years, grades 9 through 12? Name anything that comes to mind — academic studies, social contacts, club and extra-curricular activities.

....

....

....

....

(2)   Which of the specific academic areas did you like best? In the columns below, name the subjects you liked in the first column and write in the second column the reasons you believe they had value to you.

Subject   Value

(Example:
    Algebra   Taught me to work out numerical
                                            problems in my head
    English   Showed me the beauty of words
                                            and how to use them to express
                                          ideas)

....

....

(2)   Favorite subjects, continued:

Subject   Value

....

....

....

....

(3)   Which subjects do you do best? In the first column below, list those subjects and then, in the second column, tell as specifically as you can what particular abilities you used to perform well in these subjects.

Subject   Ability

(Example:

   English   Able to express myself clearly in
                                                    writing

   Spanish   Able to memorize new vocabulary,
                                                    ear for language inflections

....

....

....

....

(4)   Which out-of-class activities did you like best during high school? Include anything you did away from the classroom regardless of whether or not it took place on the school grounds or was sponsored by the school. Tell specifically what you liked best about each activity under the column labelled "Value".

Activity   Value

(Example:

   Reading psychological   Helped me to understand human
     novels   behavior)

....

....

....

....

(5)   Which out-of-class activities did you do best? For what special talents
        were you known by your peers? What specific ability was represented
        by this talent? Use the columns below to review these activities and
        abilities.

Activity   Ability

(Example:
     Assisted in coaching local   Accurate memory for facts and
        little league team   figures, rules and regulations)

....

....

....

....

....

Now look at the Values and Abilities you have identified for yourself in the five
questions. You will use some of this information later in the PATH program to
help you evaluate career possibilities.

From these Values and Abilities, select those you think may be relevant to your
career potential and enter them in the boxes below. Enter only those Values and
Abilities which you feel are as strong now as they were during high school and
which have relevance for a possible future career.

VALUES	ABILITIES
....	....
....	....
....	....
....	....
....	....
....	....
....	....

Exercise 5: COLLEGE EDUCATION

Part One: *Choosing a Liberal Arts Major*

Although it is not possible to make a choice of major field that is entirely fool-proof, the following kinds of questions should help you to consider the most important issues that are involved.

Name your present or intended major(s): ....

Present Considerations:

(1) Is this a major field that I will enjoy for its own intrinsic value? Explain, if necessary.

....

....

....

(2) Is this a major field in which I expect to perform well? Explain.

....

....

....

(3) Do I like and respect most of the faculty members in this department?
Explain.

....

....

....

....

(4) Am I keeping my options open to other departments? That is, am I taking
courses in other areas in case I may want to switch from this major field
to another? Explain.

....

....

....

What are these other possible major fields?

....

....

(5) Do I find myself seeking out other students and faculty in this department for
informal discussions and other interactions? Explain.

....

....

....

....

If you can answer YES to most or all of these
questions, then you are studying or intending
to enter a major field that is a desirable and
sensible choice for you. If there are one or
more resounding NO answers to these questions, then you had better reconsider the major
that you have chosen.

<u>Future Considerations</u>

(1) Do I understand what kinds of graduate study and employment are possible if I major in this particular field? Explain.

....

....

....

Name some of the possibilities.

....

....

(2) Will this major help me to acquire the pre-requisites necessary for the kind of graduate study I may be considering? Explain.

....

....

....

(3) Will this major help to prepare me for a particular field of employment I may be intending to enter? Explain.

....

....

....

If you must answer NO to one or more of these questions, then you should reconsider the vocational implications of your present or intended field of study.

Look through the list of major fields of study on the following page. The list is not complete but it does include most of the majors which are typically open to a student at a liberal arts college. Be sure to add any majors at your college that are not included here, if they interest you.

Evaluate each major according to its (a) Present Appeal; and (b) Relationship to your Future Goals. The term "Future Goals" can be interpreted more broadly than "Vocation" here because your choice of courses may have some direct bearing upon future goals that are not necessarily vocational.

The degrees of immediate and future importance which you assign to these major fields should give you some idea of how to compare the possibilities for your choice of a major. Weighing present enjoyment and future practicality with each other is no easy matter, and there certainly is no way to combine the factors numerically although you should be able to eliminate most of the major fields through this kind of analysis. However, the eventual commitment to a major field is still a highly personal process and very subjective at that. Your liking for a particular professor or desire for a certain sequence of courses may sway your decision even though other factors seem to point elsewhere. Or, if your college provides the freedom, you might develop your own interdisciplinary major based upon a theme which incorporates areas of learning from several different departments.

Score Each Major Field as follows:

1 = No interest at all

2 = Of some interest

3 = Desirable

4 = Highly desirable

Major Field	Present Appeal	Future Goals	Major Field	Present Appeal	Future Goals
American studies	.....	....	Music	....	....
Biology	....	....	Philosophy	....	....
Chemistry	....	....	Physics	....	....
Classical Studies	......	....	Polit. Science	....	....
Economics	....	....	Psychology	....	....
Fine Arts	....	....	Religion	....	....
Geology	....	....	Russian – Soviet		
History	....	....	Area Studies	....	....
Internat. studies	....	....	Sociology	....	....
Mathematics	....	....	South Asian		
Modern languages			Area Studies	....	....
French	....	....	Theatre & Drama	....	....
German	....	....	Education	....	....
Spanish	....	....	Other:		
Russian	....	....	....	....	....

Part Two: *Reviewing College Activities*

(1)   During a typical week at college, how do you apportion your free time? The question refers specifically to the hours over which you have free choice (outside of classes, laboratories, sleeping, eating, etc.). In the columns below list the activities, the approximate number of hours spent and the value you place on each activity.

Activity	No. Hrs./Wk	Value
(Example:		
Studying	30	competition
Playing tennis	5	physical exercise
Unassigned reading	15	drama
Tutoring math	5	teaching experience
Talking with friends	10	exchange of ideas
Band practice	2	musical teamwork)
....	....	....
....	....	....
....	....	....
....	....	....
....	....	....
....	....	....
....	....	....

(2)   What academic subjects do you like best in college? Consider specifically what you like best about each of the subjects and indicate this as a value in the columns that follow.

Academic Subject	Value
(Example:	
English literature	Exposure to writing skills of great authors
Analytic geometry	Develop ability to solve numerical problems)
....	....
....	....
....	....
....	....

(3)   What academic subjects do you feel that you do best in college? Do not look only at your grades; judge your performance according to your own standards. What particular abilities of yours contribute most to your high performance?

<u>Academic Subject</u>   <u>Ability</u>

(Example:
   Chemistry   Able to work numerical problems quickly
   Psychology   Understand results of research)

....

....

....

....

(4)   For what non-academic talents are you best known by your peers in college? Refer to any sort of activity that takes place outside the classroom regardless of whether or not it is formally sponsored by the college. List these non-academic talents below and try to determine the underlying abilities which contribute to your recognized accomplishment.

<u>Non-Academic Talents</u>   <u>Ability</u>

(Example:
   Sportswriting   Good command of vocabulary
   Card playing   Memory for numbers in sequence)

....

....

....

Now review all of the Values and Abilities you have identified for yourself in this exercise and select those which you believe may be relevant to possible careers and list them in the boxes below.

───VALUES───	───ABILITIES───

Part Three: *Graduate School Inquiry*

More and more these days, the graduates of liberal arts colleges find their way into graduate programs of various kinds. Some go immediately after their undergraduate education while others do different things for a few years and then return for advanced study. One of the vital questions is: If I am going to enroll in an advanced degree program someday, when should I do it?

(1)   What are the advantages, as you see them, of going to graduate or professional school immediately after getting your B. A. or B. S. degree?

(a) ....

....

(b) ....

....

(c) ....

....

(2)   What are the advantages of waiting two to five years before entering graduate school?

(a) ....

....

(b) ....

....

(c) ....

....

(You may want to read again pages 14 through 16 in Section I before filling in the above questions for a discussion of the advantages and disadvantages of going to graduate school immediately after college.)

The following questions might best be answered after you have visited a campus where there is a graduate program of interest to you. Use the following standard format of questions whenever you have the opportunity to talk with faculty and/or students in a graduate department:

What will I be doing three to five years after I complete my graduate program?
It pays to find out what kinds of employment are most frequently taken by graduates of the program you are considering. Visit the school and ask some of the near-graduates what they expect to be doing after they graduate.

Attrition
Do students of this graduate department frequently fail to complete their degree programs? Once again, this is not something you will learn from the catalog or the department brochure. Visit the campus and ask both faculty and students.

Depth in the faculty
How many faculty members does the department have? Does the department's reputation rest heavily upon the shoulders of just one or two professors? What if they should go elsewhere?

Diversity in the faculty
Is there a variety of points of view in the department, or are most of the faculty members' approach to the discipline rather single-minded? Would you rather be a disciple or develop your own approach to the field?

Faculty publications
What have the faculty members published lately? This will give you an idea of whether the faculty's interests are similar to your own. In many cases, what the professor publishes is what he spends the most time talking about, both in and out of the classroom.

Availability of Faculty
Are there several big names on the faculty? If so, ask the students how often they actually see or talk with these people. Would you be likely to work with the big name on a research project, see him only in class, or just hear about him occasionally?

Internships and Assistantships
Does the program have any planned practical experiences? If so, where would you be likely to work and what would you do?

Fellowships and Funds
How much fellowship money is available? How many students receive fellowships? Are you likely to be among the lucky few?

A. C. E. Ratings of Graduate Programs *
>   The highest ranked graduate departments in each of 36 disciplines has been
>   published by the American Council on Education. This study, and its ratings,
>   has been disputed by some, so you should read it cautiously; the best use
>   these ratings serve for you is to indicate certain schools that are likely to
>   have respectable programs in your chosen field.

Ph. D. Production
>   How many Ph. D.'s has this department produced yearly? What is the
>   average length of time it takes to complete the degree?

Assistance in finding a job
>   What percentage of graduates and degree candidates in this department
>   succeed in finding employment? To what extent is the department helpful
>   in enabling the graduate to find suitable work?

Admissions Preferences
>   Does the department prefer to have their applicants fresh out of undergraduate
>   school? Or, do they tend to prefer applicants having work experience
>   relevant to their field?

Versatility
>   To what extent can you use the degree from this department to get into
>   other kinds of work? Is there much latitude for applying this degree to
>   other fields?

A Rating of Graduate Programs by Kenneth D. Roose and Charles J. Anderson. American Council on Education, 1970.

Exercise 6: ENJOYABLE ACTIVITIES

Part One: *Enjoyable Activities*

(1)   In Exercises 4 and 5 you had an opportunity to identify those activities which you have enjoyed most in the past and those you are enjoying while you are in college. Now consider what kinds of things you would like to do that you have not done before, if you were suddenly given complete freedom of choice to do whatever your heart desires for the next twelve months. What activities would you choose and how would you apportion your time?

For each activity, indicate what you like best, or feel is most important, about the activity and indicate this as a corresponding "value."

Activity	Time	Value
(Example:		
Foreign travel	6 mos.	Meet a wide range of people
Run cross-country races	weekends	Build physical stamina
Recreation leader for poor children	6 mos.	Help prevent neighborhood hostilities
Study stock market	eves.	Learn how to develop financial security)

....

....

....

....

(1)   − Continued:

Activity   Time   Value

....

....

....

....

....

....

(2)   Now review the Values you have indicated. Some of them may be relevant
to your career aspirations. Select those which you feel you will want to satisfy
in your career and write them in the box below. We shall make use of these
Values in later exercises of the program.

```
┌────────────────VALUES────────────────┐
│                                        │
│   ...................................  │
│                                        │
│   ...................................  │
│                                        │
│   ...................................  │
│                                        │
│   ...................................  │
│                                        │
│   ...................................  │
│                                        │
│   ...................................  │
│                                        │
│   ...................................  │
│                                        │
│   ...................................  │
│                                        │
└────────────────────────────────────────┘
```

Group Exercise

To the Group Facilitator:

1. Divide the group into sub-groups of four people each. Assign the people on a random basis so that no individual has an opportunity to choose his partners.

2. Ask each sub-group member to write all of his "Enjoyable Activities" on a large sketch pad.

3. One at a time, each member of the sub-group should —

    (a) Display his "Enjoyable Activities" to the other three members of the group

    (b) Explain any of these "Enjoyable Activities" which are not readily understood from the label he has given

4. Immediately after a given member has displayed and explained his "Enjoyable Activities," the other three members of the group should help him to extract Values from his list by interpreting the Values which they believe are inherent in the activities described.

5. Group members should encourage clarification by asking the Focus Person questions about his "Enjoyable Activities."

    Example: "What kinds of historical novels do you enjoy most?"

             "What is it that you value most about cross-country jogging?"

6. After exchanging views with group members, the Focus Person makes the final decision regarding which Values can be extracted from his enjoyable activities.

Part Two: *"I Want to Work With People"*

You may have always assumed that you like working with people because your social contacts have usually been pleasant. Here is a chance to test just how much you want to work with people, to what extent, and in what capacity.

Check whichever of the following activities appeal to you:

. . . . . Influence the attitudes, ideas of others

. . . . . Gather information through direct contact with people

. . . . . Help people with personal problems

. . . . . Instruct other people in various tasks or skills

. . . . . Supervise others in their work

. . . . . Manage the work of others, be responsible for their output, even though not in direct contact as a supervisor

. . . . . Confront others, present them with difficult decisions

. . . . . Investigate people by obtaining information about them

. . . . . Provide service to others

. . . . . Mediate between contending parties

. . . . . Organize others; bring people together in cooperative efforts

. . . . . Make decisions about others

. . . . . Socialize with people on a regular basis

. . . . . Understand people and study their behavior

Check one or more of the following statements if they apply to you:

. . . . . I want to be part of a working team.

. . . . . I want to have people seek out my help or services, come to me.

. . . . . I want to seek out other people, go to them.

. . . . . I want to see different people every day that I work.

. . . . . I want to work with the same people for a long period of time.

. . . . . I want a lot of contact with a small number of people.

. . . . . I want brief (one-time) contacts with a large number of people.

. . . . . I do not mind being interrupted by people, to be on call as their needs require.

. . . . . I like to be able to regulate my own hours, decide when people will see me and when I can get away from them.

. . . . . I want to get to know a group of people through regular contact (e. g., shopkeeper).

If a new program of some kind were being developed, which of the following roles would you prefer? Check more than one, if desired.

..... I would want to design (create) the program from the start.

..... I would want to translate the program into a plan of operation.

..... I would want to sell the value of the program to potential users.

..... I would want to conduct the program myself.

..... I would want to manage others who operate the program.

Describe the kinds of people with whom you would most like to be involved in your work. What kinds of people would you prefer for your colleagues and co-workers? What kinds of people would you like to provide a product or service for? Describe these people in terms of personal characteristics, not simply labels. For example:

Do not say — "I want to work with engineers."

Instead, say — "I like people who are strongly oriented toward getting the job done. It would make me happier if they did not talk much on the job. I also like people who are oriented toward learning; that is, they go out of their way to learn something new in their work."

I LIKE PEOPLE WHO ....

....

....

....

....

....

Describe the kinds of people with whom you definitely do not want to be involved in your work:

I DO NOT LIKE PEOPLE WHO ....

....

....

....

....

My values are my personal decisions regarding what is most important in life.

Exercise 7: TRADITIONAL AMERICAN VALUES

Read over the following list of "Traditional American Values" (goals and attitudes which are socially approved in our American culture) and check those which you consider important in your life.

...... Get ahead

...... Be honest

...... Participate in government

...... Work hard

...... Be clean

...... Honor one's parents

...... Be loyal to your country

...... Live to the fullest

...... Pursue happiness

...... Accrue goods and wealth

...... Become educated

...... Be religious

...... Know the right people

...... Live in the right places

...... Be productive

...... Help your fellow man

...... Be tolerant

...... Explore new horizons

...... Play to win

...... Be independent

...... Obey the law

...... Influence other countries to become democratic

...... Identify with a cause

...... Know your heritage

...... Build things

...... Save time

...... Find a better way

...... Take pride in your community

...... Stand up for what you think is right

This exercise is adapted from "Traditional American Values: Intergroup Confrontation" in *The 1973 Annual Handbook for Group Facilitators*, edited by John E. Jones and J. William Pfeiffer. Iowa City, Iowa: University Associates.

(1) Now select three of these traditional values which are most important to you and rank them #1, #2, and #3 — with #1 as the most important. Write the number in front of your check mark.

(2) Why did you rank these three values the highest? Explain.

#1 ....

#2 ....

#3 ....

(3) Who influenced you most in your selection of values (parents, teachers, friends)?

....

....

....

(4) Where did your values come from (reading, example, religious training, peer group pressure)?

....

....

....

(5) Which three of these traditional values are most likely to be importantly related to the work that you will do someday? Explain.

(a) ....

(b) ....

(c) ....

List those Values from page 71 which you feel will be important in your choice of a career.

┌──────────────VALUES──────────────┐
│ .... │
│ .... │
│ .... │
│ .... │
│ .... │
└─────────────────────────────────┘

The prestige that I assign to an occupational title may reflect certain needs that I hope to fulfill in my own career.

Exercise 8: OCCUPATIONAL PRESTIGE

Part One: *Ranking Occupations*

Rank all fifteen of the following occupations according to the relative importance (prestige) that <u>you</u> attach to each. Place a number "1" in front of the occupation that <u>you</u> believe is most important and carry through to the least important, in your view, as number "15":

<u>Your Rank</u>	<u>Name of Occupation</u>
. . . .	Author of novels
. . . .	Newspaper columnist
. . . .	Policeman
. . . .	Banker
. . . .	U. S. Supreme Court Justice
. . . .	Lawyer
. . . .	Undertaker
. . . .	State Governor
. . . .	Sociologist
. . . .	Scientist
. . . .	Public School Teacher
. . . .	Dentist
. . . .	Psychologist
. . . .	College Professor
. . . .	Physician

Now compare your rankings with those of the general population.

(1)   U. S. Supreme Court Justice
(2)   Physician
(3)   Scientist
(4)   State Governor
(5)   College Professor
(6)   Lawyer
(7)   Dentist
(8)   Psychologist
(9)   Banker
(10)   Sociologist
(11)   Public School Teacher
(12)   Author of novels
(13)   Undertaker
(14)   Newspaper columnist
(15)   Policeman

Which of these occupations do you rate at least two places more important than the rankings by the general population? Comment on the difference in rank.

Name of Occupation	Your Rank	Gen. Pop. Rank	Comment
....	....	....	....
....	....	....	....
....	....	....	....
....	....	....	....
....	....	....	....
....	....	....	....

What specifically do you value most in the occupations to which you assigned a higher ranking? Remember that your unusually high ranking probably means that you attribute a particular worth to this occupation that is not perceived by most other people. List these values in the spaces below.

Name of Occupation	Difference in Ranking	Value
(Example:		
Author of novels	Ranked #3 vs. #12	Ability to express ideas and understand human nature
Policeman	Ranked #6 vs. #15	Enforcing laws protects the freedom of all citizens)
....	....	....
....	....	....

Name of Occupation	Difference in Ranking	Value
....	....	....
....	....	....
....	....	....

In the box below, make a note of those values indicated above which you feel may be relevant to your future career. Do not be too concerned at this point about what your career is going to be. Just consider whether a value is important enough to be considered in your career decision and write it in the box.

```
┌─────────────VALUES─────────────┐
│                                │
│  ............................  │
│                                │
│  ............................  │
│                                │
│  ............................  │
│                                │
│  ............................  │
│                                │
│  ............................  │
│                                │
│  ............................  │
│                                │
│  ............................  │
│                                │
└────────────────────────────────┘
```

The preceding section of this Exercise 8 was adapted from "Consensus Seeking" in *Structured Experiences for Human Relations Training*, vol. II by Pfeiffer and Jones, University Associates, Iowa City, Iowa, 1970.

The "General Population" rankings are based on N.O.R.C. prestige scores from R. V. Hodge, P. M. Siegel, and P. H. Rossi, "Occupational Prestige in the United States," 1925-1963, pgs. 322-334 in R. Bendix and S. M. Lipset (eds.) *Class Status and Power*, 2nd edition. New York, The Free Press, 1966.

Part Two: *Influence of Significant Others*

An individual's choices are often influenced by the people with whom he lives or those whom he sees on a regular basis. Many vocational development theorists believe that the expectations of others, role models, and social class factors weigh heavily upon you in your choice of a vocation. How often do you think to yourself —

"Will this be a respectable choice in the eyes of those who know me?"

(1) Which of the following people has had a noticeable effect upon the vocational choices that you are considering at this point? Write "strong," "marginal," or "none."

....	Mother	....	Relative(s)
....	Father	....	Other adults
....	Brother(s)		High School teacher
	Sister(s)	....	Counselor
....	Minister	....	Other students
....	Close friend(s)	....	College professor

(2) What vocation do your parents want for you, if they had their choice?

....

....

(3) What vocation do your friends and peers think that you are best suited for?

....

....

(4) To what extent are you tending to perpetuate the family history in your likely choice of a vocation? To what extent are you reacting against the family's vocational history?

....

....

(6) Tell about the person or people who have most influenced your thinking about possible vocations (including negative as well as positive influence).

....

....

....

The world is filled with people trying to do what they most enjoy, after 5:00 PM. (Richard Bolles)

Exercise 9: WORK VALUES

Part One: *Rating Satisfactions from Work*

(1)   The following list describes a wide variety of satisfactions that people obtain from their jobs. Look at the definitions of these various satisfactions and rate the degree of importance that you would assign to each for yourself, using the scale below:

1 = Not important at all

2 = Not very important

3 = Reasonably important

4 = Very important in my choice of career

...... <u>Help Society</u>: Do something to contribute to the betterment of the world I live in.

...... <u>Help Others</u>: Be involved in helping other people in a direct way, either individually or in small groups.

...... <u>Public Contact</u>: Have a lot of day-to-day contact with people.

...... <u>Work with Others</u>: Have close working relationships with a group; work as a team toward common goals.

...... <u>Affiliation</u>: Be recognized as a member of a particular organization.

...... <u>Friendships</u>: Develop close personal relationships with people as a result of my work activities.

...... <u>Competition</u>: Engage in activities which pit my abilities against others where there are clear win-and-lose outcomes.

77

...... Make Decisions: Have the power to decide courses of action, policies, etc.

...... Work under Pressure: Work in situations where time pressure is prevalent and/or the quality of my work is judged critically by supervisors, customers or others.

...... Power and Authority: Control the work activities or (partially) the destinies of other people.

...... Influence People: Be in a position to change attitudes or opinions of other people.

...... Work Alone: Do projects by myself, without any significant amount of contact with others.

...... Knowledge: Engage myself in the pursuit of knowledge, truth and understanding.

...... Intellectual Status: Be regarded as a person of high intellectual prowess or as one who is an acknowledged "expert" in a given field.

...... Artistic Creativity: Engage in creative work in any of several art forms.

...... Creativity (general): Create new ideas, programs, organizational structures or anything else not following a format previously developed by others.

...... Aesthetics: Be involved in studying or appreciating the beauty of things, ideas, etc.

...... Supervision: Have a job in which I am directly responsible for the work done by others.

...... Change and Variety: Have work responsibilities which frequently change in their content and setting.

...... Precision Work: Work in situations where there is very little tolerance for error.

...... Stability: Have a work routine and job duties that are largely predictable and not likely to change over a long period of time.

...... Security: Be assured of keeping my job and a reasonable financial reward.

...... Fast Pace: Work in circumstances where there is a high pace of activity, work must be done rapidly

...... Recognition: Be recognized for the quality of my work in some visible or public way.

...... Excitement: Experience a high degree of (or frequent) excitement in the course of my work.

...... Adventure: Have work duties which involve frequent risk-taking.

...... Profit, Gain: Have a strong likelihood of accumulating large amounts of money or other material gain.

...... Independence: Be able to determine the nature of my work without significant direction from others; not have to do what others tell me to.

. . . . . . <u>Moral Fulfillment</u>: Feel that my work is contributing significantly to a set of moral standards which I feel are very important.

. . . . . . <u>Location</u>: Find a place to live (town, geographical area) which is conducive to my life style and affords me the opportunity to do the things I enjoy most.

. . . . . . <u>Community</u>: Live in a town or city where I can get involved in community affairs.

. . . . . . <u>Physical Challenge</u>: Have a job that makes physical demands which I would find rewarding.

. . . . . . <u>Time Freedom</u>: Have work responsibilities which I can work at according to my own time schedule; no specific working hours required.

(2) Now choose four of these Work Values which are the most important to you and write them in the box below. Each of these values will be relevant to the career exploration that you will do in later exercises. If you can think of any other work values (desired satisfactions) that are not included in the list above and which are especially important to you, add them to the four values you list in the box.

(Example: Recognition
Help Others
Creativity
Independence)

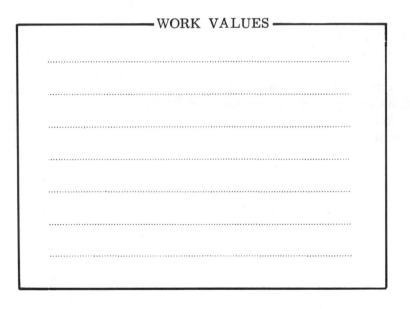

WORK VALUES

Part Two: *Things I'd Like to Change*

1. Look through the areas of "change" listed below. Assume that you would have complete freedom to work in any of these areas. Where would you spend your time? Imagine that you had 100 weeks to distribute among these areas.

2. As you make your choices, stress the things that <u>you</u> would actually like to work on <u>yourself</u>, not things that you'd simply like to see others change.

3. After you've distributed your 100 weeks, decide what Values are inherent in the three or four areas where you allotted your greatest number of weeks. Write these Values in the box below.

<u>I would like to . . .</u>   <u>No. Weeks</u>

(a) Clean up the environment   . . . .
(b) Introduce political reform   . . . .
(c) Restore economic stability   . . . .
(d) Teach people to communicate better   . . . .
(e) Reduce violence   . . . .
(f) Build better houses   . . . .
(g) Increase respect for the arts   . . . .
(h) Reduce self-defeating behavior   . . . .
(i) Create more interesting jobs for people   . . . .
(j) Improve family relationships   . . . .
(k) Invent better products for the home   . . . .
(l) Reduce unhealthful behavior   . . . .
(m) Reform the schools   . . . .
(n) Reduce crippling diseases   . . . .
(o) Develop new energy sources   . . . .
(p) Expand people's sensitivity to religious ideas   . . . .
(q) Restore historical-cultural continuity in the U. S. A.   . . . .
(r) Build safer vehicles for transportation   . . . .
(s) Aid the world food problem   . . . .
(t) Work toward peace, here and in other countries   . . . .

It is okay to assign zero weight to some of these categories.

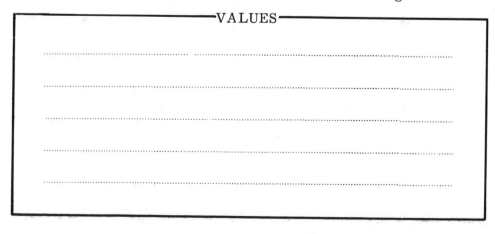

Group Exercise

<u>Instructions to the Group Facilitator:</u>

1. Divide the entire group into sub-groups of four people each; assign the people on a random basis so that no individual has any influence over the other people in his/her sub-group.

2. Ask each person to tell the other three about the three things he/she would most like to change in the world.

3. Immediately after the Focus Person tells his/her three highest priority topics of change, the other three group members should actively question the Focus Person to determine what core values are represented by his/her choices.

4. The Focus Person and the group members exchange views regarding what these values should be called and they eventually try to reach consensus.

5. The Focus Person has the final say in the choice of Values labels to be added to his or her list.

10

10

10

10

Exercise 10: UNIQUE EXPERIENCES

(1)   Reflect broadly upon experiences you have had, things that you have done, and people to whom you have been exposed during your lifetime. What things have you done that not many others have done? What kinds of activities have you engaged in more often than most people your age?

In casting back through your memory, it may prove helpful to consider the following categories of experience:

(a) Jobs you have held

(b) Hobbies you have practiced

(c) Special school projects you have completed

(d) Careers or jobs experienced by members of your family, relatives, or close friends, from which you have learned a great deal

(e) How you spent your Saturdays during high school when you had no obligations during the day

(f) Summertime activities

(g) Hometown institutions or experiences that are not available in most other towns

(h) Unusual people you have known

(i) Things you have done frequently during "alone" time

This review can be carried into any realm of your life experience, and can reach as far back into the past as you please.

List below all of these activities or experiences which are at least uncommon compared to people in your age group.

(2)   Beside each experience that you list, write whatever ability you feel you have obtained as a result of this experience. That is, indicate whatever advantage or insight you feel that you have gained from the experience which you would not otherwise possess.

Experience	Ability
(Example: Read psychological novels	Acquired insight into levels of mental health
Camp counselor summers	Learned to relate well to adolescents
Sports spectator	Developed an eye for the dramatic)
....	....
....	....
....	....
....	....
....	....
....	....

(3)   Now consider which of the "abilities" you have listed above might be relevant to the work you hope to do in the future. That is, which of the above experiences might be applied to a potential career?   List the appropriate abilities in the box below. We will use them in a later exercise.

```
┌──────────────ABILITIES──────────────┐
│                                      │
│  ..................................  │
│                                      │
│  ..................................  │
│                                      │
│  ..................................  │
│                                      │
│  ..................................  │
│                                      │
└──────────────────────────────────────┘
```

(See page 87 for a Group Exercise which may be adapted to this Exercise.)

CORE PROGRAM

Exercise 11: ACHIEVEMENTS

List ten Achievements of yours, large and small, things you have done during the past ten years that you thought were important and represented a sense of some accomplishment to you regardless of whether or not they were formally recognized. Refer each achievement to an actual behavior, something that you did. Do not use personal characteristics or traits as examples of achievement.

The emphasis should be upon events that you really felt good about. These should be "achievements" in your own eyes. Do not be concerned about whether or not these achievements meet a standard of excellence compared to other people. The examples below will cue you regarding the range and nature of activities that you might want to include.

"Achievement" Examples:

I got a summer job as a survey interviewer.

I helped my five-year old brother learn to tell time.

I organized a carnival at my high school.

I learned how to climb a mountain with a team and equipment.

I designed a floor plan for a new house.

I created a market for artistic photography in my community.

This exercise has been adapted with permission from the DIG program developed by Richard Gummere at Columbia University.

Achievement No. 1: ....

....

Achievement No. 2: ....

....

Achievement No. 3: ....

....

Achievement No. 4: ....

....

Achievement No. 5: ....

....

Achievement No. 6: ....

....

Achievement No. 7: ....

....

Achievement No. 8: ....

....

Achievement No. 9: ....

....

Achievement No. 10: ....

....

Now that you have listed your Achievements, consider what particular qualities you possessed which enabled you to accomplish these particular tasks. Don't be shy about this. Every task requires that an individual have certain attributes to get the job done. Use the examples as guides.

You will note that in the examples two different Achievements can have a similar underlying Ability ("organize" well). This may or may not be true for your particular items but do not be reluctant to mark the same Ability for two different items if this is the case. Now list below, in abbreviated form, the Achievements you have described and pair them with the underlying Abilities which enabled you to complete the tasks.

Achievement

(Example:
  Find summer job

Help brother tell time
Plan carnival
Mountain climbing

Ability

Organize and ferret out inform-
  ation
Communicate with children
Organize details
Resistance to physical hardship

Achievement

....

....

....

....

....

....

....

....

....

Ability

....

....

....

....

....

....

....

....

....

Which of the above Abilities would you regard as having potential for your career possibilities? That is, which abilities might have the strongest application in the work that you hope to do? Write no more than three of these abilities in box below.

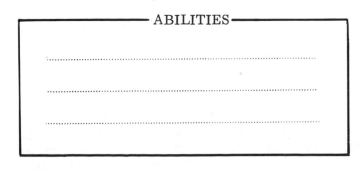

ABILITIES

Group Exercise

To the Group Facilitator:

1. Divide the group into sub-groups of four people each; assign these people to each sub-group on a random basis so that no individual can influence the people with whom he is placed.

2. Ask each participant to write descriptive headings or labels for all of his or her Achievements on a large sketch pad.

3. Each participant then describes to his three sub-group partners what kinds of things he did in order to accomplish each of the particular Achievements.

4. Immediately following an individual's description of his or her Achievements and the behaviors which contributed to these achievements, the other three group members attempt to interpret the Abilities which the Focus Person was using in each of these accomplishments.

5. The Focus Person and his partners then exchange views about the specific nature of the Abilities which underlie the Achievements being discussed. The three respondents should ask helpful questions; such as —

> "When you organized the fund-raising drive for your church, did you do much of the direct canvassing yourself?"

> "When you studied the ecology of the rivers in your home county, did you rely primarily upon your scientific background or did you spend time organizing the scientific talents of other people?"

6. Once the partners have exchanged views and all clarifying questions have been introduced, the Focus Person makes the final determination about the Abilities that he or she will extract from the original Achievements.

(Note: This Group Exercise can be adapted in similar fashion to the previous exercise, Exercise No. 10, "Unique Experiences")

12

12

Exercise 12: STRANGE TOWN EXPERIENCE

Imagine you have been told that you must move to a strange town, a place where nobody knows you and no one can obtain access to your past. You come to the town without any credentials, evidence of educational achievements, employment certificate or such. You must find work but the only way that you can convince an employer of your qualifications is to demonstrate your talents or talk him into believing that you can do a particular job well.

Assume that there is no such thing in this town as civil service tests, union membership or other formal credentials required for employment. The purpose here is to help you identify abilities that you possess which do not depend upon knowing anyone or belonging to any particular group of supportive individuals.

(1)　Organizations

Name three kinds of organizations which you would seek out in order to obtain initial information. (Example: Chamber of Commerce)

....

....

....

(2)　People

Name three kinds of people you would seek out to obtain preliminary information about the town, possible jobs, etc. (Examples: Cab drivers, policemen, town officials, school teachers, barbers, etc.)

(3)   <u>Yellow Pages</u>

Look through the listing of categories in the Yellow Pages of the local telephone directory (see page 134 of this book) and choose at least three categories which would seem to have likely prospects for you in job-hunting.

....

....

(4)   <u>Talents</u>

What talents do you possess which could be used on a pretty immediate basis in order to seek employment? Name these most readily available talents even if there is no guarantee that there would be a market for them.

....

....

....

(5)   <u>Potential Talents</u>

What talents do you possess which have the potential for future employ-ability but would require some time to develop.

....

....

(6)   Which of the following areas of talent would you be likely to depend upon in the Strange Town?

	Very Likely	Somewhat Likely	Not at all
(a) Work with my hands	....	....	....
(b) Supervise or manage others	....	....	....
(c) Influence other people	....	....	....
(d) Technical skill with machines	....	....	....
(e) Verbal skills	....	....	....
(f) Mathematical skills	....	....	....
(g) Service to the public	....	....	....

(7)   All things considered, what are the specific ways in which you believe you would be most likely to earn a living in a Strange Town?

....

....

....

....

....

Are there any talents which you have uncovered here, not mentioned in previous exercises, that you think may have an application to your future career? If so, write them in the Abilities box below.

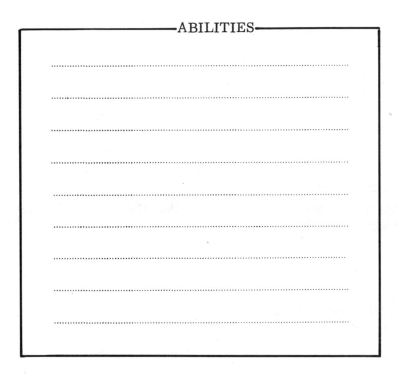

My failures may represent unfinished business. They are moments when I disappointed myself, because I felt that I could have done better. In time, I hope to turn these failures around and make them into successes.

Exercise 13: FAILURES

List six experiences or activities in which you have had some feelings of failure, having done less than you felt you were capable of doing. Small as well as large disappointments should be included. Once again, the failures that went largely unrecognized by others are just as important here. Link each of these six experiences to some behavior — a thing that you actually did rather than a personal trait or characteristic.

You should focus here on events that resulted from your own shortcomings rather than those outcomes which were a result of forces not under your control. Your emphasis should be upon your disappointment with yourself, not upon how your performance compared with external standards of excellence or the performance of other people. "Failure" should not be invested with overtones of crisis; it should simply represent an event in which you felt you were capable of doing better but did not.

See next page for examples of failures.

Failure No. 1: ....

....

Failure No. 2: ....

....

Failure No. 3: ....

....

Failure No. 4: ....

....

Failure No. 5: ....

....

Failure No. 6: ....

....

In looking back at these Failures, can you discern particular qualities in your behavior which were largely responsible for the outcome? Which of these qualities do you feel that you have improved today or could improve upon if you were given the opportunity?

The examples provide some clues about how your particular failures might be interpreted. Write an abbreviated description of your Failures in the spaces below and tie each failure to some quality responsible at the time.

Failure   Quality Responsible

(Examples:
Lost a journalism award   Lacked verbal fluency
Did a poor job teaching
  sports at summer camp   Unable to give clear directions
Failed to read several books
  I had planned to read   Slow reader
Failed to save money for a
  vacation trip   Poor self-discipline)

....

....

....

....

....

....

....

....

You may feel that there are certain qualities noted above that you have since improved so that now you can replace them with abilities which are assets. If you feel there are any of the failure qualities which have been improved to abilities which might help you in your future work, list them in the box below.

(Examples:

Improved oral and written communication
Took course in speed reading)

14

14 **Exercise 14: SELF-EVALUATION of ABILITIES**

Part One: *Evaluating Abilities*

14 (1)   What are the things that you do best? Refer to the broadest possible range of your experience. Do not be concerned about whether your answers have any particular relationship to careers. Of all the things that you do or have done before, what do you perform with the greatest skill? Some of these may be talents which come naturally to you and thus may be difficult for you to notice in yourself. Name one or more and describe them as specifically as you can.

(a) ....

(b) ....

14 (c) ....

(d) ....

(2)   Now look through the Abilities categories which are defined on the following pages and evaluate yourself on each of these according to the following scale:

14

1 = No ability here at all

2 = Enough ability to get by with help from others

3 = Some ability

4 = Definite, strong ability in this area

When evaluating your abilities, do not compare yourself with any particular reference group such as other students in your college, all college students, the general population, or such. Just rate yourself according to your best estimate of your capability.

Self-Rating	VERBAL-PERSUASIVE

.... <u>Writing</u>: express myself well in written forms of communication

.... <u>Talking</u>: relate easily with people in ordinary conversational settings

.... <u>Speaking</u>: able to deliver a talk or address to an audience

.... <u>Persuading</u>: able to convince others to believe something that I hold to be true

.... <u>Selling</u>: able to convince others to buy a product that I am selling

.... <u>Dramatics</u>: able to portray ideas or stories in a dramatic format

.... <u>Negotiating</u>: able to bargain or discuss with a view toward reaching agreement

SOCIAL

.... <u>Social ease</u>: relate easily in situations which are primarily social in nature; i.e., parties, receptions, etc.

.... <u>Deal with public</u>: relate on a continual basis with people who come to an establishment for information, service or help, including a broad cross-section of people

.... <u>Good appearance</u>: dress presentably and appropriately for a variety of interpersonal situations or group occasions

.... <u>Deal with negative feedback</u>: able to cope with criticism

NUMERICAL

.... <u>Computational speed</u>: able to manipulate numerical data rapidly without the aid of a mechanical device, demonstrating considerable accuracy in the process

.... <u>Work with numerical data</u>: comfortable with large amounts of quantitative data, compiling, interpreting, presenting such data

.... <u>Solve quantitative problems</u>: able to reason quantitatively so that problems having numerical solutions can be solved without the aid of a computer or other mechanical equipment

.... <u>Computer use</u>: able to use electronic computers to solve quantitative problems; knowledge of programming, computer capabilities, etc.

INVESTIGATIVE

. . . .   Scientific curiosity: ability to learn scientific phenomena and investigate events which may lead to such learning

. . . .   Research: gather information in a systematic way for a particular field of knowledge in order to establish certain facts or principles

. . . .   Technical work: work easily with practical, mechanical or industrial aspects of a particular science, profession or craft

MANUAL-PHYSICAL

. . . .   Mechanical reasoning: able to understand the ways that machinery or tools operate and the relationships between mechanical operations

. . . .   Manual dexterity: skill in using one's hands or body

. . . .   Spatial perception: able to judge the relationships of objects in space, to judge sizes and shapes, manipulate them mentally and visualize the effects of putting them together or of turning them over or around*

. . . .   Physical stamina: physical resistance to fatigue, hardship and illness

. . . .   Outdoor work: familiar with the outdoors, ability to work outdoors without encountering obstacles or knowledge deficiencies

CREATIVE

. . . .   Artistic: keenly sensitive to aesthetic values, able to create works of art

. . . .   Imaginative with things: able to create new ideas and forms with various physical objects

. . . .   Imaginative with ideas: able to create new ideas and programs through conceiving existing elements of behavior in new ways; able to merge abstract ideas in new ways

WORKING WITH OTHERS

. . . .   Supervising: able to oversee, manage or direct work of others

. . . .   Teaching: able to help others learn how to do or understand something; able to provide knowledge or insight

---

*Donald E. Super and J. O. Crites, *Appraising Vocational Fitness*, Rev. Ed. New York: Harper Brothers, 1962, p. 287.

. . . .   <u>Coaching</u>: able to instruct or train an individual to improve his or her performance in a specific subject area

. . . .   <u>Counseling</u>: able to engage in a direct helping relationship with another individual in situations where the person's concern is not solvable through direct information-giving or advice

MANAGERIAL

. . . .   <u>Organization and planning</u>: able to develop a program project or set of ideas through systematic preparation and arrangement of tasks, coordinating the people and resources necessary to put a plan into effect

. . . .   <u>Orderliness</u>: able to arrange items in a systematic, regular fashion so that such items or information can be readily used or retrieved with a minimum of difficulty

. . . .   <u>Handle details</u>: able to work with a great variety and/or volume of information without losing track of any items in the total situation; comfortable with small informational tasks that are part of the larger project responsibility

. . . .   <u>Make decisions</u>: comfortable in making judgments or reaching conclusions about matters which require specific action; able to accept the responsibility for the consequences of such actions

(3)   Of the Abilities you have rated for yourself, which do you believe represent your most prominent strengths? Refer both to those you rated for yourself on the 1 to 4 scale and those which you described in Question No. (1). Choose whichever of these are your most outstanding Abilities and write them in the box below.

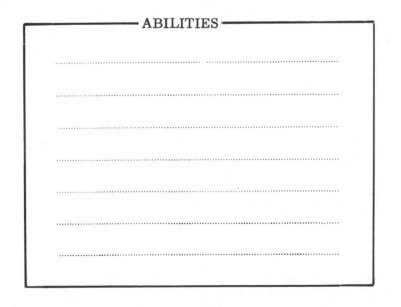

Part Two: *What Is the Best You Ever Did?*

1. Reflect upon the <u>best</u> you ever did in each of the following categories.

2. Consider what Abilities you were using to accomplish each of these "best" experiences. You may use the inventory of Abilities in Part One of this exercise or define other Abilities that seem appropriate.

<u>The BEST ...</u>   <u>ABILITY</u>

Speech (talk) I ever gave ....

....

Paper I ever wrote ....

....

Letter I ever wrote ....

....

Poem I ever wrote............................   ....

....

School project I ever constructed ....

....

Personal relationship I ever had ....

....

Trip I ever planned ....

....

Decision I ever made............................   ....

....

"Cause" I ever fought for ....

....

Coursework I ever did in college (high school)   ....

....

Test I ever made an "A" on ....

....

The BEST ...   ABILITY

Position of responsibility I ever held ....

....

Team I was ever a member of ....

....

Hobby I ever had ....

....

Problem I ever solved ....

....

Research I ever did ....

....

Performance I ever gave ....

....

Job I ever performed ....

....

Thing I ever taught to someone ....

....

Leadership role I ever fulfilled ....

....

3. Which of the Abilities identified here are most prominent to you, either because they occur frequently in your "best" categories or because they identify strengths that seem especially applicable to your future work possibilities? List these prominent Abilities in the box below.

```
┌──────────────── ABILITIES ────────────────┐
│                                            │
│       ....................................  │
│                                            │
│       ....................................  │
│                                            │
│       ....................................  │
│                                            │
│       ....................................  │
│                                            │
│       ....................................  │
│                                            │
└────────────────────────────────────────────┘
```

15

15

Exercise 15: TRIAL OCCUPATIONS—SELECTION

Part One: *Choosing Trial Occupations*

Now it is time to explore a broad variety of occupational titles, to consider some of the standard options which exist in the world of work, and judge which of these seem potentially suitable. Do not consider that these choices of Trial Occupations will be binding in any way; they simply serve the purpose of giving you some ideas with which to experiment and perhaps some building blocks for developing a fuller idea of your career.

You may choose your Trial Occupations through one or more of the following three methods, preferably all three if you have the time.

(1) Look through the Occupational Roster on the following pages and choose those Trial Occupations whose definitions seem to offer the best prospects for —

(a) Making use of your talents; and
(b) Satisfying your work values.

(2) Look through several standard reference books of occupational information such as those noted below and select occupational titles that seem to have the potential for satisfying your abilities and work values.

Dictionary of Occupational Titles *
Occupational Outlook Handbook *
Encyclopedia of Careers *
Occupational Thesaurus *

* See Bibliography in the Appendix for complete reference information.

(3) Imagine occupational titles that you believe may exist somewhere in the world of work (most everything does) and which would have the greatest promise for making use of your talents and satisfying your values. Create whatever title seems appropriate to you. Refer back to Exercise Two for any "career fantasies" you may have written there which seem suitable as Trial Occupations here.

<u>Choose at least five Trial Occupations but limit yourself to no more than ten.</u>

* * *

List your Trial Occupations in the column below and consider carefully your reason for choosing them. Then, in the second column write what you value most about the Trial Occupation selected, using the examples as a guide.

Trial Occupation	Value
(Examples:	
Psychologist	Opportunity to study human behavior
Actuary	Enjoy doing numerical problems
Market Researcher	Analyze consumer motivation
English teacher	Study great literature
Journalist	Live close to where the action is)

List your Trial Occupations again on the following page, examining them this time for abilities you believe you might capitalize upon in each occupation. What do you feel you could do well in each? Be as specific as possible, using the examples as a guide.

Trial Occupation	Abilities
(Examples:	
Psychologist	Knowledge of psychopathology
Actuary	Able to solve numerical problems quickly
Market Researcher	Orderly habits for organizing data and compiling results
English teacher	Have read widely and know how to recognize literary style
Journalist	Able to express ideas concisely)

....

....

....

....

....

....

....

....

....

Now select the four Values and four Abilities from your lists which are most likely to be relevant to your future career and write them in the boxes:

┌─── VALUES ──────────────┐   ┌─── ABILITIES ────────────┐
│ .... │   │ .... │
│ .... │   │ .... │
│ .... │   │ .... │
│ .... │   │ .... │
└──────────────────────────┘   └──────────────────────────┘

Part Two: *Occupational Roster*

Definitions for the following occupations have been abridged from two U.S. Labor Department publications: Dictionary of Occupational Titles, 1965, Volume I, Definitions of Titles, 3rd edition, U.S. Government Printing Office, Washington, D.C., and Occupational Outlook Handbook, 1972-73, Bureau of Labor Statistics, Washington, D.C.

ACCOUNTANT: Applies principles of accounting to install and maintain operation of general accounting systems; designs new systems or modifies existing system to provide records of assets, liabilities, and financial transactions of establishment; audits contracts, orders and vouchers, and prepares reports which substantiate individual transactions before their settlement.

ACTUARY: Applies knowledge of mathematics, probability, statistics, principles of finance, and business to problems of life, health, social and casualty insurance, annuities and pensions; determines mortality, accident, sickness, disability and retirement rates.

ADVERTISING WORKER: Includes executives responsible for planning and overall supervision of advertisements, copywriters who write the text, artists who prepare the illustrations and layout specialists who put copy and illustrations into the most attractive arrangement possible.

ANTHROPOLOGIST: Makes comparative studies of origin, evolution, and races of man, cultures they have created, and man's distribution and physical characteristics.

ARCHITECT: Plans and designs private residences, office buildings, theaters, public buildings, factories, and other structures, and organizes services necessary for construction.

ASTRONOMER: Observes and interprets celestial phenomena and relates research to basic scientific knowledge or to practical problems, such as navigation.

BIOLOGIST: Studies origin, relationship, development, anatomy, functions, and other basic principles of plant and animal life; may specialize in research centering around a particular plant, animal or aspect of biology.

BUYER: Purchases merchandise for resale; selects and orders merchandise from showings of manufacturing representatives, basing selection on nature of clientele, demand for specific merchandise and experience as buyer.

CASEWORKER: Counsels and aids individuals and families requiring assistance of social service agency; interviews clients with problems such as personal and family adjustments, finances, employment, and physical and mental impairments, to determine nature and degree of problem.

CHEMIST: Performs chemical tests, qualitative and quantitative chemical analyses, or conducts chemical experiments in laboratories for quality of process control or to develop new products or new knowledge.

CLINICAL PSYCHOLOGIST: Diagnoses mental and emotional disorders of individuals, and administers programs of treatment; interviews patients in clinics, hospitals, prisons and other institutions, and studies medical and social case histories.

COMMERCIAL ARTIST (ILLUSTRATOR): Draws and paints illustrations for advertisements, books, magazines, posters, billboards and catalogs.

COPY WRITER: Consults with Account Executive and media and marketing representatives to obtain information about product or service and to discuss style and length of advertising copy, considering budget and media limitations; writes original copy for newspapers, magazines, billboards, and transportation advertising; writes scripts for radio and television advertising.

CREDIT ANALYST: Analyzes credit data to estimate degree of risk involved in extending credit or lending money to firms or individuals, and prepares reports of findings; contacts banks, trade and credit associations, salesmen, and others to obtain credit information.

CURATOR (MUSEUM): Administers affairs of museum and conducts scientific research programs; directs activities concerned with instructional, research, and public service objectives of institutions; interprets and assists in formulating museum or herbarium administrative policies; supervises curatorial, preparatory, and clerical staff; administers exchange of loan collections; obtains, develops and organizes new collections to build up and improve educational and research facilities.

DANCER: Performs dances alone, with partner, or in groups, such as corps de ballet or chorus ensemble, to entertain audience.

DIETITIAN: Plans and directs food service programs in hospitals, schools, restaurants, and other public or private institutions; plans menus and diets providing required food and nutrients to feed individuals and groups.

ECONOMIST: Conducts research, prepares reports, and formulates plans to aid in solution of economic problems arising from production and distribution of goods and services.

EDITOR, BOOK: Interviews author, suggests changes in book manuscripts, and negotiates with authors regarding details of publication, such as royalties to be paid, publication date, and number of copies to be printed, according to knowledge of production requirements and estimation of public demand for book.

FASHION COORDINATOR: Promotes new fashions and coordinates promotional activities, such as fashion shows, to induce consumer acceptance.

FINANCIAL ANALYST: Conducts statistical analyses of information affecting investment programs of public, industrial, and financial institutions, such as banks, insurance companies and brokerage and investment houses.

FORESTER: Manages and develops forest lands and their resources for economic and recreational purposes; plans and directs projects in forestation and reforestation; maps forest areas, estimates standing timber and future growth and manages timber sales.

GEOGRAPHER: Studies nature and use of areas of earth's surface, relating and interpreting interactions of physical and cultural phenomena; conducts research on physical and climatic aspects of area or region.

GEOLOGIST: Studies composition, structure, and history of earth's crust; examines rocks, minerals and fossil remains to identify and determine sequence of processes affecting development of earth.

GUIDANCE COUNSELOR: Concerned with educational, vocational and social development of students in schools and colleges; counselors work with students, both individually and in groups, as well as with teachers, other school personnel, parents and community agencies.

HISTORIAN: Prepares in narrative, brief, or outline form chronological account or record of past or current events dealing with some phase of human activity, either in terms of individuals, or social, ethnic, political, or geographic groupings.

HOME ECONOMIST: Develops, interprets, and applies principles of home-making to promote health and welfare of individuals and families; advises homemakers in selection and utilization of household equipment, food and clothing, and interprets homemakers' needs to manufacturers of household products.

HOSPITAL ADMINISTRATOR: Administers and coordinates activities of hospital personnel to promote care of sick and injured, furtherance of scientific knowledge, development of preventative medicine, advancement of medical and vocational rehabilitation, and participation in and promotion of community health and welfare.

INDUSTRIAL DESIGNER: Designs form of products to be manufactured and associated packaging and trademarks; sketches design or products, such as furniture, lamps, motor vehicles, radio cabinets, and household appliances, taking into consideration appearance for sales appeal, service-ability in adapting design to function, price, costs, and methods of production and specifications stipulated by clients.

INSURANCE UNDERWRITER: Decides the acceptability of various types of risks by analyzing information contained in insurance applications, reports of safety engineers, and actuarial studies (reports describing the probability of insured loss).

INTERIOR DESIGNER AND DECORATOR: Plans and designs artistic interiors for homes, hotels, ships, commercial and institutional structures, and other establishments; analyzes functional requirements, moods, and purpose of furnishing interior, based on clients needs and preferences.

INTERPRETER: Translates spoken passages of foreign language into specified language; may be designated according to language or languages interpreted.

LABOR-RELATIONS SPECIALIST: Serves as specialist on labor management relations, representing either management or labor union; studies and interprets collective bargaining agreements and current labor market conditions to assist in establishing policies and operating procedures; represents management or labor in contract negotiations and conciliation and arbitration procedures.

LANDSCAPE ARCHITECT: Plans and designs development of land areas for such projects as parks and other recreational facilities, airports, highways, parkways, hospitals, schools, land subdivisions, and commercial, industrial and residential sites.

LAWYER: Conducts criminal and civil lawsuits, draws up legal documents, advises clients as to legal rights, and practices other phases of law; gathers evidence in divorce, civil, criminal, and other cases to formulate defense or to initiate legal action.

LIBRARIAN: Maintains library collection of books, periodicals, documents, films, recordings, and other materials, and assists groups and individuals to locate and obtain materials.

LIFE INSURANCE UNDERWRITER: Solicits and sells all types of life insurance, based on client's present insurance and government benefits, to establish plan for financial security; advises client concerning life insurance, pensions, taxation and family finance.

MANUFACTURERS' REPRESENTATIVE: Sells single, allied, diversified or multi-line products to wholesalers or other customers for one or more manufacturers on commission basis.

MARKET RESEARCH ANALYST: Researches market conditions in local, regional, or national area to determine potential sales of a product or service; examines and analyzes statistical data on past sales and wholesale or retail trade trends to forecast future sales trends.

MATHEMATICIAN: Conducts research in fundamental mathematics and in application of mathematical techniques to science, management, and other fields, and solves or directs solutions to problems in various fields by mathematical methods.

METEOROLOGIST: Studies and interprets atmospheric conditions and related meteorological data to forecast immediate and long range changes in weather.

NEWS REPORTER: Collects and analyzes facts about news-worthy events by interview, investigation or observation, and writes newspaper stories conforming to prescribed editorial techniques and format; reports to scene or beat or special assignment, as directed; interviews persons and observes events to obtain and verify story facts, and to develop leads for future news items.

NURSE, PROFESSIONAL: (A term applied to persons meeting educational, legal, and training requirements to practice as professional nurses, as required by a State Board of Nursing.) Performs acts requiring substantial specialized judgment and skill in observation, care and counsel of ill, injured, or infirm persons and in promotion of health and prevention of illness.

OCCUPATIONAL THERAPIST: Plans, organizes, and participates in medically oriented occupational program in hospital or similar institution to rehabilitate patients who are physically or mentally ill; utilizes creative and manual arts, recreational, educational, and social activities, prevocational evaluations and training in everyday activities, such as personal care and homemaking.

PAROLE OFFICER: Engages in activities related to conditional release of juvenile or adult offenders from correctional institutions; establishes relationship with offenders and familiarizes himself with offender's social history prior to and during institutionalization.

PERSONNEL MANAGER: Plans and carries out policies relating to all phases of personnel activities; organizes recruitment, selection, and training procedures. and directs activities of subordinates directly concerned; confers with company and union officials to establish pension and insurance plans, workmen's compensation policies, and similar functions.

PHARMACIST: Compounds and dispenses medications, following prescriptions issued by physicians, dentists, or other authorized medical practitioners; weighs, measures and mixes drugs and other medicinal compounds.

PHARMACOLOGIST: Studies effects of drugs, gases, dusts, and other minerals on tissues and physiological processes of animals and human beings; experiments with animals, such as rats, guinea pigs, and mice to determine reactions of drugs and other substances on the functioning of organs and tissues, noting effects on circulation, respiration, digestion or other vital processes.

PHOTOGRAPHER, COMMERCIAL: Photographs persons, motion-picture sets, merchandise, exteriors and interiors, machinery, and fashions to be used in advertising and selling.

PHYSICAL THERAPIST: Treats patients with disabilities, disorders and injuries to relieve pain, develop or restore function, and maintain maximum performance, using physical means, such as exercise, massage, heat, water, light and electricity as prescribed by physician.

PHYSICIAN: (A term for persons with degree of doctor of medicine who diagnose and treat disease and disorders of the human body.) Examines patients, utilizing all types of medical equipment, instruments and tests, following standard medical procedures.

PHYSICIST: Conducts research into phases of physical phenomena, develops theories and laws on basis of observation and experiments, and devises methods to apply laws and theories of physics to industry, medicine and other fields.

PHYSIOLOGIST: Conducts research on cellular structure and organ-system functions of plants and animals; studies growth, respiration, circulation, excretion, movement, reproduction, and other functions of plants and animals under normal and abnormal conditions.

POLITICAL SCIENTIST: Conducts research into origin, development, operation, and interrelationships of political institutions, studies phenomena of political behavior and develops political theory.

PROGRAMMER, BUSINESS: Converts symbolic statement of business problems to detailed, logical flow charts for coding into computer language and solution by means of automatic data-processing equipment.

PUBLIC RELATIONS WORKER: Plans and conducts public relations programs designed to procure publicity for groups, organizations, or institutions through such media as magazines, newspapers, radio and television; selects and assembles publicity material that accords with organizational policy; writes news releases and submits photographs to newspapers.

PURCHASING AGENT: Purchases machinery, equipment, tools, raw materials, parts, services, and supplies necessary for operation of an organization, such as an industrial establishment, public utility or government unit.

RADIO-TV ANNOUNCER: Introduces various types of radio or television programs, interviews guests, and acts as master of ceremonies; reads news flashes, identifies station by giving call letters; gives necessary network cues to control room so that selected stations connected by telephone lines may receive intended programs.

RANGE MANAGER: Conducts research in range problems to provide sustained production of forage, livestock and wildlife; studies range lands to determine best grazing seasons and number and kind of livestock that can be most profitably grazed.

RECREATION LEADER: Conducts recreation activities with assigned groups in public department of voluntary agency; organizes, promotes and develops interest in activities, such as arts and crafts, sports, games, music, dramatics, social recreation, camping and hobbies.

SALESMAN, REAL ESTATE: Rents, buys and sells property for clients on commission basis; studies property listings to become familiar with properties for sale; reviews trade journals to keep informed of marketing conditions and property values; interviews prospective clients to solicit listings.

SANITARIAN: Specialist in environmental health; assures the cleanliness and safety of the food people eat, the liquids they drink and the air they breathe; perform a broad range of duties.

SECURITIES TRADER: Performs securities investment and counseling service for a bank and its customers; studies financial background and future trends of stocks and bonds; advises bank officials and customers regarding investments.

SOCIOLOGIST: Conducts research into origin and development of groups of human beings and patterns of culture and social organization which have arisen out of group life in society.

SOIL CONSERVATIONIST: Plans and develops coordinated practices for soil-erosion control, moisture conservation and sound land use; conducts surveys and investigations on erosion and on preventative measures needed; plans soil management practices, such as crop rotation, strip cropping, contour plowing, and reforestation as related to soil and water conservation.

SPEECH PATHOLOGIST: Diagnoses, treats and performs research related to speech and language problems; diagnoses speech and language disorders by evaluating etiology; treats language and speech impairments, such as aphasia, stuttering and articulatory problems or organic and non-organic etiology.

STATISTICIAN, APPLIED: Plans surveys and collects, organizes, interprets, summarizes and analyzes numerical data on sampling of complete enumeration bases, applying statistical theory and methods to provide usable information in scientific and other fields.

SYSTEMS ANALYST: Analyzes business problems, such as development of integrated production, inventory control and cost analysis system, to refine its formulation and convert it to programmable form for application to electronic data-processing system.

TEACHER, ELEMENTARY: Teaches elementary school pupils academic, social, and manipulative skills in rural or urban communities; prepares teaching outline for course of study.

TEACHER, HANDICAPPED CHILDREN: Teaches handicapped pupils in elementary and secondary grades, evaluating pupils' abilities in order to determine training programs that will result in maximum progress; observes pupils to determine physical limitations and plans academic and recreational programs to meet individual needs.

TEACHER, MENTALLY RETARDED: Teaches mentally retarded children basic academic subjects in schools, centers and institutions; plans courses of study according to pupils' levels of learning; conducts activities in subjects, such as music, art, crafts, and physical education, to stimulate and develop interests, abilities, manual skills and coordination.

TEACHER, SECONDARY: Instructs students in one or more subjects, such as English, mathematics, or social studies, in private, religious, or public secondary school (high school); instructs pupils through lectures, demonstrations and audiovisual aids.

TECHNICAL WRITER: Organizes, writes and edits material about science and technology so that it is in a form most useful to those who need to use it, be it a technician or repairman, a scientist or engineer, an executive or a housewife.

URBAN PLANNER: Develops comprehensive plans and programs for utilization of land and physical facilities of cities, counties, and metropolitan areas; compiles and analyzes data on economic, social, and physical factors affecting land use, and prepares or requisitions graphic and narrative reports on data.

VETERINARIAN: Diagnoses and treats diseases and disorders of animals; determines nature of disease or injury and treats animal surgically or medically.

Part Three: *Occupational Data Sheet*

The Occupational Data Sheet is an in-detail assessment of a particular Occupation as it relates to you, your needs, your abilities, and your unique characteristics. If you can complete all of the questions, you will know a great deal about how you might expect to relate to that kind of work, the reasons why you would like to do it or the reasons why you might not like it.

At this moment, you probably do not have many of the answers to these questions. Hence, now is the time to get out and meet people in the occupation and talk to them about their experiences. You must "interview" them, just as though their jobs were being considered by you as candidates for possible hiring. Do you want to "hire" that person's job for yourself, or would you prefer to go elsewhere? Ask them questions which appear directly on the Occupational Data Sheet.

Name of Occupation: ....

What specific kinds of duties are performed?

....

....

....

What kind of work would I be doing, if I were hired as a "no experience" college graduate?

....

....

....

Name three different kinds of organizations which employ people in this occupation:

1. ....

2. ....

3. ....

What might my expected sequence of positions be, if I were to enter this occupation and make it a career?

1. ....

2. ....

3. ....

What are the educational requirements for this occupation?

....

....

What level of demand is exerted upon the employee? To what degree is there "pressure" on this job?

....

....

....

Roughly, how many hours of work per week are expected or desirable for peak performance? How many nights per week will be consumed by job responsibilities?

....

....

....

Would my work in this occupation be likely to have any noticeable effects upon my health?

....

....

Which of my abilities or personal qualities would be noticeably important in this occupation?

....

....

....

Which of my deficiencies would make it difficult for me to succeed?

....

....

....

What major satisfactions would I derive from this occupation?

....

....

....

Which of my personal needs would definitely <u>not</u> be satisfied?

....

....

....

Is there a prevalent "life style" among people who populate this occupation?
If so, I would describe it this way:

....

....

....

....

....

....

....

....

....

....

An occupation is of interest to me only in terms of how well it satisfies my values and draws upon my most prominent talents.

Exercise 16: TRIAL OCCUPATIONS—COMPARISON

Part One: *Values Groupings*

(1)   During several prior exercises, you have decided upon values that you feel are likely to be important to you in your future career. It is now time to summarize these values and see what they may mean to your career decision process.

Refer to the VALUES boxes in Exercises 4, 5, 6, 7, 8, 9 and 15 and list below all of the values you wrote in these boxes.

(Examples:
>   Work out numerical problems in my head
>   Beauty of words and how to use them to express ideas
>   Understand human behavior
>   Physical exercise
>   Drama
>   Teaching experience
>   Exchange of ideas
>   Musical teamwork
>   Exposure to writing skills of great authors
>   Solve numerical problems
>   Meet a wide range of people
>   Build physical stamina
>   Help prevent neighborhood hostilities
>   Learn how to develop financial security
>   Recognition
>   Help Others
>   Creativity

113

Independence
Opportunity to study human behavior
Enjoy doing numerical problems
Analyze consumer motivation
Study great literature
Live close to where the action is   )

VALUES

(2)   <u>Grouping your values</u>

As you review the values which you have listed, you will probably find similarities among many of them. Combine any values which are reasonably similar into a "Values Grouping." The example below will serve as a guide for the development of your Values Groupings.

Once you have made your Values Groupings, decide which five of these groupings are the most important and mark them for future attention with a check, dash, star, asterisk, or other notation. Select your five most important Values Groupings according to these criteria:

(a) How many different times was this Value cited in previous exercises?

(b) How much importance do you attach to the Value in this grouping with regard to possible future careers?

<u>Values</u>   <u>Values Grouping</u>

(Examples:
Work out numerical problems   Work with numerical data and problem-
Solve numerical problems   solving
Enjoy doing numerical problems

Beauty of words and how to use   Study and emulate great writers and
  them to express ideas   their styles
Exposure to writing skills of
  great authors
Study great literature

Understand human behavior   Understand human behavior and its
Study human behavior   related pathology
Analyze consumer motivation   )

.... (1) ....

....

....

....

....

.... (2) ....

....

....

....

Values	Values Groupings
....	(3) ....
....	....
....	....
....	....
....	(4) ....
....	....
....	....
....	....
....	(5) ....
....	....
....	....
....	....

(3) Comparing Trial Occupations in Terms of Your Values

Now you will evaluate your Trial Occupations by examining the degree to which each Trial Occupation can satisfy your prominent values. In the Table on page 118, list the five top Values Groupings from Question 2 on the top line of the Data Table. In the lefthand column, list the Trial Occupations you selected in Exercise 15.

Consider each Value Grouping as it might relate to each of the Trial Occupations. Is this Value one which you would expect to have satisfied in the particular occupation? Evaluate each Trial Occupation X Value cell of the table, according to the following scale:

YES Trial Occupation would satisfy this value very well
? Trial Occupation might satisfy the Value reasonably well
NO Trial Occupation would not satisfy the Value at all

Example of Data Table #1:

 If "working with numerical data" is one of your prominent Values, and the Trial Occupation is Actuary, one would expect that your Value would be well satisfied by this Trial Occupation and you would mark YES in the appropriate space on the Data Table.

 Complete the Data Table for each combination of Trial Occupation and Value according to the scale suggested. The final result may look something like the following example:

Value Grouping

Trial Occupations	1 Help Others	2 Numerical Data	3 Understand Human Behavior	4 Write with Style	5 Physical Fitness
Counselor	Yes	No	Yes	Yes	?
Actuary	?	Yes	No	No	No
Investment Analyst	Yes	Yes	No	?	No
Marketing Research	No	Yes	Yes	?	No
Magazine Writer	No	No	Yes	Yes	No
Private Business	No	Yes	No	No	Yes
English Professor	Yes	No	?	Yes	Yes

 We shall make no attempt to assemble and make a combined evaluation of all the data you give for a particular Trial Occupation; nor will we add up the Yes, No and Question Mark answers in order to reach a final rating because we do not want to introduce closure to your career development process in this exercise.

 The only purpose of the Data Table is to help you think through the ways in which each Trial Occupation might satisfy, ignore, or even inhibit the expression of your most prominent career-related Values.

 You are now ready to turn the page and fill in your own Data Table for Value Groupings and Trial Occupations.

 (You will notice in the example above that each Value is satisfied by several different Trial Occupations and that each Trial Occupation satisfies several different Values. This diversity should also be true for the Values and Trial Occupations you indicate in your own Data Table.)

DATA TABLE #1

Value Groupings

Trial Occupations	1	2	3	4	5

Part Two: *Abilities Groupings*

(4)   During several previous exercises you have decided upon Abilities that you believe you are likely to utilize in your future career. It is now time to summarize these Abilities and recognize what meaning they may have for your career decision process.

Refer to the ABILITIES boxes in Exercises 4, 5, 10, 11, 12, 14 and 15, where you indicated career-relevant abilities at the end of each exercise. List all of these Abilities below in the space provided on the next page.

(Examples:
   Express myself clearly in writing
   Memorize vocabulary words easily
   Do mathematical problems with great speed
   Familiar with nature
   Work numerical problems quickly
   Understand results of research experiments

Memory for numbers in sequence
Able to analyze numerical data
Familiar with good writing styles
Sensitive to mental health
Relate well to adolescents
Have an eye for the dramatic
Have knowledge of clinical psychology
Able to organize details
Patient with children
Know how to ferret out information
Sense what is marketable
Fluent in speaking publicly
Able to work in a team)

ABILITIES

....

....

....

....

....

....

....

....

....

....

....

....

....

....

....

....

(5)   <u>Grouping Your Abilities</u> *

As you review the Abilities which you have listed, you will find that many of them are similar enough to be grouped together. Combine any Abilities which are reasonably similar into an "Abilities Grouping." The example below will serve as a guide for the development of your Abilities Groupings.

Once you have determined your Abilities Groupings, decide which five of these are the most important, and mark them for future attention with a check, dash, star, asterisk, or other notation. Select your five most important Abilities Groupings according to these criteria:

(a) How many times was this Ability cited in previous exercises?

(b) How much importance do you attach to the Ability in this grouping with regard to possible future careers?

<u>Abilities</u>   <u>Abilities Groupings</u>

(Examples:

Do math problems with great speed   Work with numerical data;
Work numerical problems quickly   solve numerical problems, etc.
Analyze numerical data

Express myself clearly in writing   Ability to write clearly,
Familiar with good writing styles   draw upon quality styles, etc.
Fluent in public speaking

Sensitive to mental health   Knowledge and sensitivity to
Knowledge of clinical psychology   problems of mental health, etc.
Relate well to adolescents

Able to organize details   Organize and analyze information
Know how to ferret out information   )

Note in the example that certain Abilities listed initially are not included in any of the Abilities Groupings. This is because some of the Abilities in the examples were not similar enough to other Abilities listed; thus, they were not considered important enough to be included in the final Abilities Groupings. You should include in the final Abilities Groupings only those Abilities which you feel are most important to your future career considerations.)

....   (1)   ....

....

....

*This procedure for grouping Abilities is similar in concept to a procedure for "Skills Clustering" developed by John C. Crystal, Crystal Management Services, Inc., McLean, Virginia.

<table>
<tr><th>Abilities</th><th>Abilities Groupings</th></tr>
</table>

Abilities	Abilities Groupings
....	(2) ....
....	....
....	....
....	....
....	(3) ....
....	....
....	....
....	(4) ....
....	....
....	....
....	(5) ....
....	....
....	....

(6)   <u>Comparing Trial Occupations in Terms of Your Abilities</u>

Once you have determined your five Abilities Groupings, list them as column headings in the Data Table #2. Then refer to the Trial Occupations that you selected in Exercise 15 and list these as row headings on the left side of the Data Table. The example will provide cues for your own Data Table.

Consider each Ability Grouping as it might relate to each of the Trial Occupations. Is this Ability one that you would expect to be able to use effectively in that particular Trial Occupation? Evaluate each Ability X Trial Occupation cell, according to the following scale:

YES   Trial Occupation would allow me to use Ability very well
  ?   Trial Occupation might allow me to use Ability reasonably well
NO   Trial Occupation would not allow me to use this Ability

(Example:

    If "writing creative prose" is one of your prominent Abilities and the Trial Occupation is Journalist, one would expect that your Ability would be at least reasonably well utilized by the Trial Occupation and that you would mark YES in the appropriate cell of the Data Table.)

    Complete the Data Table for each combination of Trial Occupation X Ability. Your final result might look something like this:

Ability Grouping

Trial Occupations	Write Prose	Work With Numbers	Counsel Others	Organize Data	Deal With Public
Counselor	Yes	No	Yes	?	?
Actuary	No	Yes	No	Yes	No
Investment Analyst	?	Yes	?	Yes	Yes
Marketing Research	Yes	Yes	No	Yes	Yes
Magazine Writer	Yes	No	No	Yes	Yes
Private Business	?	Yes	No	Yes	Yes
English Professor	Yes	No	Yes	No	No

    You will notice in the Example that each Ability is satisfied by several different Trial Occupations and that each Trial Occupation satisfies several different Abilities. This diversity should also exist for the Abilities and Trial Occupations which you indicate in your own Data Table.

DATA TABLE #2

Abilities Grouping

Trial
Occupations

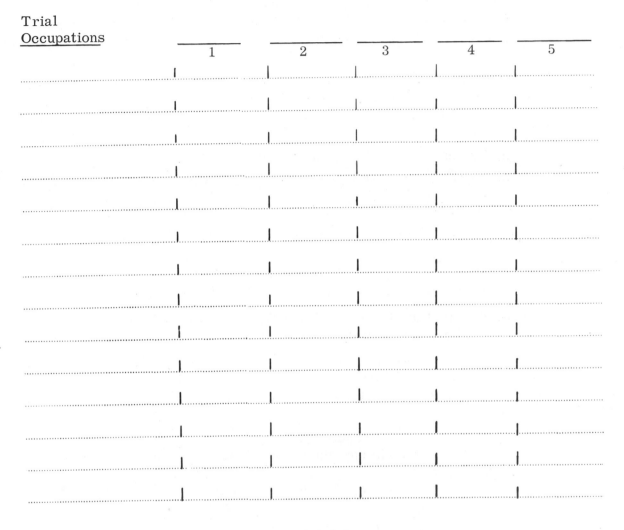

	1	2	3	4	5

* * * *

We shall make no attempt to assemble and make a combined evaluation of all the data you have given for a particular Trial Occupation in the Data Table. We do not want to add up the pluses and minuses in order to reach a final rating for each Trial Occupation because we do not want to introduce closure to the career development process during this exercise. The only purpose of this Data Table is to help you think through the ways in which each Trial Occupation might satisfy, ignore, or even inhibit the use of your most prominent career-related Abilities.

Rather than use the Data Table to rate Trial Occupations against each we shall introduce the next exercise ("Creating My Own Career") as a more satisfactory solution to the problem of deciding upon a career direction.

Group Exercise

<u>To the Group Facilitator:</u>

1. Divide the entire group into sub-groups of four people each; assign these people on a random basis so that no individual has an opportunity to influence the three other members with whom he or she will be placed.

2. Ask each sub-group participant to display on a large sketch pad his/her entire lists of Values and Abilities which he/she has extracted from all of the prior exercises. The sketch pad should show:

    (a) The entire list of Values groupings on the left side;

    (b) The entire list of Abilities groupings on the right side.

3. One person at a time, members of the sub-group should:

    (a) Display the sketch pad to the other three members;

    (b) Ask the other members to name Trial Occupations which they believe would best be suited to the Focus Person's lists of Values and Abilities groupings;

    (c) Withhold the identity of the Trial Occupations they have chosen from the previous exercise (#15).

4. Immediately following the members' guesses about the Focus Person's suitable trial occupations, there should be an exchange of views regarding these interpretations of the Focus Person's sketch pad:

    (a) The three respondents should ask the Focus Person questions which may clarify the choices of Trial Occupations;
        Example — "If you were an Architect, would you get satisfaction from applying your artistic ability to the design of new buildings?"

    (b) The Focus Person should give feedback after he has heard the group members guesses about his Trial Occupations; to what extent does he/she feel they are on target? To what extent have they misinterpreted his/her occupational needs?

    (c) This exchange of interpretations should continue until all four members of the sub-group have reached some consensus regarding at least three trial occupations for the Focus Person. The latter shall have the final say in this matter.

Work is a euphemism for everything you've ever done . . .
leisure decisions and work decisions may be one and the same.
(Richard Bolles)

Exercise 17: CREATING MY OWN CAREER—
BASED ON VALUES

(1)   Once again, list below the five Values Groupings which you determined for yourself in Exercise 16.

Values Groupings

1 ....

2 ....

3 ....

4 ....

5 ....

(2)   Now, consider how all of these Values might be satisfied within a single career. What sort of work might draw together all of the Values that you regard as most important? Think carefully about this and do your best to describe as specifically as possible the kind of "creative" career that emerges from the list of Values above. The following examples will help you.

Example #1

Values: Help others, work with numerical data, earn much money, write
        with style, maintain physical fitness

I want to work in the business world where I can solve problems for customers which involve the analysis and interpretation of numerical data.

I want to use this information in a direct helping relationship with the customers and do it in a way that my performance will be rewarded by financial benefits. In conjunction with these responsibilities, I want to write about the things that I do, in a popular journal which would have a business audience. I want to work in a setting and/or location where I will have sufficient opportunity to exercise in the outdoors.

Example #2

Values: Scientific knowledge, influence people, use foreign languages, business involvement, photography

I want to be involved with the production of scientific equipment which can be sold to people in other countries. In such a role, I could help to identify the needs of international customers, using photographic techniques to convey ideas of production improvement from one country to another. I would hope to have direct contact with the potential buyers and be required to use my language facility.

Example #3

Values: Work with my hands, be involved with dramatics, be involved with antiques, sell things and ideas

I want to build a store that will house many antiques which I can offer for resale. In addition to this, I want to use the antiques to stage dramatic productions which depict the history of the times when these items were being used. Thus, my store would be a merchandising outlet during the daytime, a theater at night.

Example #4

Values: Work with numbers, be close to professional sports, teach on on a one-to-one basis (consulting), do research

I want to do statistical analysis of professional sports teams in order to help them improve their performance. In this regard, I would like to be an independent contractor for hire by various teams who would use me on a consulting basis. In this respect, I would do research on the team's performance, then analyze data leading to recommendations, and then meet personally with team managers to instruct them about best use of the information.

In creating your career, dream as broadly and wildly as you wish. Do not be concerned about whether or not such a career actually exists. Stretch your concept of a career to include activities which may seem as if they do not belong together.

On the next page you have a chance to write your ideas for a career based on your Value Groupings.

<u>A Career Created From All My Values Priorities</u>

18

Exercise 18: CREATING MY OWN CAREER—
BASED ON ABILITIES

(1)   Once again, list below the five Abilities Groupings which you determined in Exercise 16. Include only those Abilities which you entered into Data Table #2 of Exercise 16.

Abilities Groupings

1 ....

2 ....

3 ....

4 ....

5 ....

(2)   Now consider how all of your prominent Abilities might be utilized within a single career. What sort of work responsibilities might draw together all of the talents that you possess? Think carefully about this and do your best to describe as specifically as possible the kind of "creative career" that might emerge from the list of Abilities above. Be as imaginative as possible.   The following examples will help you.

Example #1

Abilities: Work with young people, building construction, speak to local
groups about community problems, manage other people.

I want to be involved with young people because I work well with them
and have a talent for directing their efforts. I also have a strong need
to work with general construction, buildings, etc. I like to manage
people, but I am even more interested in having some say about community housing problems because I think that I understand what's wrong
with the town we live in and have some ideas about how we could improve people's housing. Perhaps I would do best working for both the
public schools and the county, teaching kids how to build houses, talking to community groups about our individual and collective housing
needs and helping the town or county decide about housing policies.

Example #2

Abilities: Knowledge of water resources, scientific knowledge of water
            pollution, numerical analysis, knowledge of boating craft.

I can apply my knowledge of pleasure-craft boating and water resources
to problems of ecology which are created by the boating industry. I
have a strong scientific background in this area and am well acquainted
with boating activities plus their effects upon natural bodies or water.
I expect that this kind of work would involve numerical studies as well.

Example #3

Abilities: Teaching, handicrafts, organizing groups of people, carpentry
            and industry design, fund raising.

I think I would do a good job of building a recreation center for people
in a community and helping to develop the staff of that center. I could
apply my abilities in constructing things, bringing a working group of
people together on the project and then teaching them how to to teach
crafts and similar skills to others.

Example #4

Abilities: Motorcycle riding, influence people, work with young people,
            community work, dramatics

My experience in cycle riding would give me a good entree with young
groups in my community and my background in dramatics would help
me to get them involved in some guerrilla theater. I think that I can
influence them to turn their attention toward constructive, community-
based activities.

Example #5

Abilities: Boating, writing, historical research, geology

I think I am uniquely suited to doing research on historical expeditions
by land and water because I have background in both long-distance
boating and the study of geological formations and I have knowledge of
the historical format of investigation and reporting. I believe that I
could write satisfactory reports of my findings for professional journals
and school textbooks.

A Career Based on My Prominent Talents

Group Exercise

To the Group Facilitator:

1. Divide the entire group into sub-groups of four people each; assign these people so that no individual has any influence upon the membership in his or her particular sub-group.

2. Ask each sub-group member to display the sketch pad showing his entire lists of Values and Abilities groupings.

3. One person at a time, each member of the sub-group should:

    (a) Display his/her sketch pad to other members.

    (b) Ask the other three members to name one or more Fantasy Careers which they believe suitable.

    (c) The Fantasy Careers should, as nearly as possible, refer to occupations which do not yet exist or are difficult to find.

    > Example — "You ought to have a job selling antiques of American folklore to people in other countries." (To capitalize on your priorities in selling, collecting antiques and foreign languages.)

    > Example — "You ought to do a quantitative study of the restoration of forest lands and design a plan which would have political acceptability." (To capitalize on your strengths in numerical reasoning, forestry, and political planning.)

    (d) The Focus Person should withhold his own description of a Fantasy Career ("Creative Careers" — Exercises 17 and 18) until he has heard the suggestions of group members.

4. The Focus Person should engage in an exchange of ideas with the three other members of the sub-group in the following ways:

    (a) Each group member responding to the Focus Person should be as specific as possible regarding Fantasy Careers.

    (b) Once the Focus Person has heard the contributions of the group members, he/she should explain how these guesses compare with the "creative careers" he/she has fashioned and why he/she defined creative careers in these ways.

    (c) All four members of the sub-group should reach some degree of consensus regarding one or more Fantasy Careers that seem most ideal for the Focus Person.

    (d) The Focus Person has the final say in this matter.

Exercise 19: POTENTIAL EMPLOYERS—SURVEY

In order to find the right kind of situations or organizations for starting your career, you should be asking yourself two key questions:

(1) What kinds of people or organizations need the <u>abilities</u> that I have to offer?

(2) What kinds of organizations are most likely to satisfy the <u>values</u> that I most desire in a career?

It will not be easy to determine the kinds of organizations which will suit you best. It will require searching, creative thinking, trial and error, and time. However, it is an effort that you must make if you are to find the people with whom you would most like to work and the work responsibilities that will satisfy you best.

Yellow Pages Listings

All that you ever really need to find prospective employers is that most readily available of resources, the Yellow Pages of the Telephone Book. Wally Segap to the rescue! Almost every type of employer in this country can be found in the Yellow Pages and the telephone company conveniently organizes them for you. There is a classification for every vocational field, and even a cross-index for locating other employer headings which may interest you.

On the following pages you will find a summary of certain employer categories which appear in the Yellow Pages of the Manhattan telephone directory. The list includes categories of employers that are the most likely to provide work opportunities of interest to college graduates.

Exercise

Choose the employer categories from the Yellow Pages classifications which seem to have good potential for satisfying the creative careers which you developed in Exercises 17 and 18. Do not be too concerned about <u>knowing</u> whether these employers would be satisfactory to you; just select the ones that you <u>guess</u> would be most appropriate. Exercise 20 will instruct you to investigate the suitability of these employers in the most effective way.

Example

(Career Objective: Solve business problems, use numerical data, be
involved in creative writing, study investments

Potential Employer Categories:
        Banks
        Business Consultants
        Investment Securities
        Management Consultants
        Insurance Companies
        Marketing Research
        Public Relations Consultants
        Publishers
        Magazines
        Economic Surveys)

List below the potential employer categories from the following list which seem appropriate for the career needs you expressed in Exercises 17 and 18.

<u>Potential Employers</u>

Yellow Pages Categories for College Graduates

Accountants — CPA's
Acoustical Contractors
Advertising Agencies
Air Line Companies
Air Pollution Control
Animal Hospitals
Architectural Consultants
Art Galleries & Dealers
Artists
Associations
Audio-Visual Consultants
Art Publishers
Antique Dealers
Actuaries
Adoption Agencies

Banks
Book Dealers — Retail
Business Consultants
Business & Trade Organizations
Building Contractors
Book Reviewers

Calculating & Statistical Services
Camps & Campgrounds
City & Town Planners
Chemists — Analytic & Consulting
Child Guidance
Church Organizations
Clinics
Clipping Bureaus
Clubs
Communications Consultants
Consulates & Other Foreign
  Government Representatives
Contractors — General
Criminologists
Credit Reporting Agencies
Color Consultants
Consumer Cooperatives

Data Processing Service
Day Nurseries
Department Stores
Drivers
Dog Breeders
Dramatic Instruction
Drug Abuse Information Centers
Display Designers

Economists
Educational Consultants
Employment Agencies
Employment Services — Government,
  Company, Fraternal, etc.
Export Managers
Engineering — Consultants
Estate Management
Educational Research
Economic Surveys
Editorial Service

Florists
Food Consultants
Foreign Marketing Consultants
Foundations
Fund Raising Organizations
Family Counselors
Food Service Management

Geologists
Government (City, State, U.S.)
Guide Service
Games & Game Supplies

Health Food Products
Historic Places
Hospitals
Home Builders
Housing Consultants
Hotel & Motel Management
Holding Companies
Home Repair & Maintenance
Horticultural Consultants

Importers
Industrial Consultants
Insurance
Interior Decorators
Investment Securities
Information Retrieval

Laboratories
Labor Relations Counselors
Lecturers — Lecture Bureaus
Libraries
Literary Agents
Library Research Service

Marriage Counselors
Magazines

Management Consultants
Marine Consultants
Marketing Research
Motion Picture Consultants
Motivation Research
Museums
Music Arrangers & Composers
Medical Research
Medical Laboratories
Motion Picture Producers
Music Bureaus

Newspapers
News Publications
Nursing Homes

Oceanographers

Personal Problems Consultants
Personnel Consultation
Pharmaceutical Products
Photographers — Commercial
Physical Therapists
Political Organizations
Printers
Proofreaders
Psychologists
Public Opinion Analysts
Public Relations Counselors
Publishers — Books
Publishers — Periodicals
Patent Searchers
Professional Organizations

Radio Audience Analysis
Real Estate
Rehabilitation Services
Restaurant Consultants
Retirement Communities
Religious Organizations
Recreation Centers
Research & Development Laboratories

Schools
Security Consultants — Protection
Senior Citizens Service Organizations
Social Service & Welfare Organizations
Speech Improvement
Stock & Bond Brokers
Sanitariums
Sanitation Consultants
Sports Promoters

Television Audience Analysis
Test Publishers
Theatrical Agencies
Tourists Information
Travel Bureaus
Tutoring
Translators & Interpreters
Travel Clubs

Veterans & Military Organizations

Writers
Weather Forecast Service

Youth Organizations & Centers

20

20

Exercise 20: POTENTIAL EMPLOYERS—EVALUATION

Part One: *Strategy During College*

You are wondering: "How can I ever find the time during college to do the kind of first-hand investigation of employers that seems to be required?"

Although summer jobs, part-time jobs, and volunteer experiences are useful strategems for getting a first-hand look at potential kinds of work, they do not provide you exposure to a sufficient range and variety of work opportunities. You must devise a way to get across-the-board exposure to a wide variety of work settings. Hence the following strategy is recommended:

(1) Turn Academic Study into a Job Survey

If your college allows any opportunity for "independent study" outside of the classroom (and most colleges do), create a project that will allow you to explore a wide range of people and jobs in the world of work.

Example: Economics — Manpower Planning

You could study the economics of manpower planning for the state in which you live. In the course of such a study, you would have to visit numerous employers at which time you could obtain information and impressions that would aid your own career development.

Example: Sociology — Worker Mobility

A sociological study of the degree to which people change their residences as a result of employment shifts and personal restlessness.

Example: Psychology — Worker Stress

A study of the psychology of stress induced by work situations, the factors which intensify or reduce such stress, etc.

Example: English — Creative Writing

Use a survey of working people as a vehicle for creating a fiction or non-fiction piece about the lives of certain people in this country.

(2) Choose a Convenient Area for Your Job Survey

Choose a nearby city, town, or county which is small enough so that you will be able to cover prospective employers on a person-to-person basis without an undue amount of travel. Make sure that the area you select has many, if not all, of the prospective employer categories you identified in Exercise 19.

(3) Use the Yellow Pages

Using the employer categories from the Yellow Pages, make a list of the names and addresses of your target employers. If you have difficulty choosing among those in a given category, you might concentrate on those which are listed in all capital letters, bold face type.

(4) Employer Directories

There are numerous specialized directories available which list hundreds of organizations that exist in a given field. Many of these provide actual names of people you can contact for job information in addition to the name of the organization, address and telephone number. A sampling of these directories is listed on pages 149-153, classified according to occupational area (i.e., Art, Advertising, Banking, Conservation, etc.).

(5) Get in the Door

By hook or crook, you must find a way to get in to talk with the people who are doing the kinds of work that interest you most. As a student who is doing an independent study, this should not be too difficult. You are only asking for a small amount of his or her time and simply want to learn about work that goes on there.

(6) Use Inquiring Reporter Form

The standard Inquiring Reporter form on page 143 will give you a framework of sample questions that you can use when you talk with an employer. You do not have to ask all of those questions and will probably not have time to do so anyway. However, remember that a form such as this will help make your interview more successful because it will cue you about exactly what to ask rather than forcing you to rely upon your memory or imagination.

When you interview an employer you are essentially trying to discover the answers to two questions:

1. Does this kind of work fit the image of what I thought (and hoped) that it would be?

If the answer to #1 is Yes —

2. How did this person get an opportunity to get into this kind of work?

(Remember, people love to talk about themselves if you will just give them the opportunity. Ask a person about the work that he or she does, the worst problems in the job and the things he or she likes best. Then sit back and be a good listener.)

(7) <u>Go to Professional Meetings</u>

In addition to the information that you can gather from having interviews with your list of prospective employers, it may be useful to learn where the people in a given profession hold their national and regional meetings, and make plans to attend. Just think — several hundred people who do the kinds of work that you want to do, all gathered in the same hotel and attending meetings together!

If you can manage to scrape up enough funds for a trip to a professional convention, the number of "information interviews" you could obtain would make the trip highly worthwhile.

(a) Using a reference book such as the <u>Occupational Outlook Handbook</u> (which is available in nearly every College Placement Office), you should be able to identify the Professional Associations which are appropriate for the kinds of employers whom you would like to meet.

(b) Another reference book, <u>The Directory of Trade and Professional Associations</u>, will tell you when and where each Professional Association holds its annual meetings and perhaps some of the regional meetings as well.

* * *

(1) Academic Topic for my "Job Survey" ....

....

(2) My Preferred Geographical Area: ....

....

(3) List of Prospects from Yellow Pages:

<u>Name of Employer</u>	Address

<u>Name of Employer</u>   <u>Address</u>

....

....

....

(4) List of Prospects from Employer Directories:

<u>Name of Employer</u>   <u>Address</u>

....

....

....

....

....

....

(5) Information-Seeking Interviews:

<u>Interview #1</u>

Title of Job: ....

Is this job as I imagined it would be? (Explain) ....

....

How did this person reach his current position? ....

....

Names of people suggested by this person for further consultation:

<u>Name of Individual</u>   <u>Employer and Address</u>   <u>Tel. No.</u>

....

....

....

....

<u>Interview #2</u>

Title of Job: ....

Is this job as I imagined it would be? (Explain) ....

....

How did this person reach his current position? ....

....

Names of people suggested by this person for further consultation:

<u>Name of Individual</u>	<u>Employer and Address</u>	<u>Tel. No.</u>
....	....	....
....	....	....
....	....	....
....	....	....

(6) Professional Associations Relevant to My Career Preferences:

<u>Name of Association</u>	<u>Time and Place of Meeting</u>
....	....
....	....
....	....
....	....
....	....
....	....
....	....
....	....
....	....
....	....

Part Two: *Strategy After College*

In addition to the suggestions in the previous section, During College, for steps to be taken, you should consider the following strategies:

(1) <u>Narrow the Geographical Area</u>

Choose a city, town, county or metropolitan area that suits you best. Select it on the basis of non-work factors, such as climate, social opportunities, friends available, etc. However, be sure that there are enough potential employers in the area who have the possibility of meeting your work needs.

(2) <u>Get an "Interim" Job</u>

Since you have little time and less money after college graduation to look around for a suitable career job, stretch the job-hunting time by obtaining an interim job. The "Interim" jobs listed at the end of this exercise are relatively easy to obtain because they require no previous experience or training; and they have the unique advantage of putting you in touch with a lot of people during the course of your duties.

Keep this kind of job as long as necessary while you are hunting down the kinds of work that you really want to do. Play this interim job for all it is worth. Talk with people who are doing things in their jobs which interest you. Poke around for job "leads" and valuable inside information. Sooner or later you will meet someone who can help you.

(3) <u>Start a Chain of Referrals</u>

Once you have talked with someone in an information-seeking interview, as you did for your academic study in the During College portion of this exercise, you should always ask, "Can you tell me the names of other people who are doing the kind of work you do and how I might get in touch with them? May I say that you suggested I contact them?"

In almost all situations, the person you have talked with will know other people in the field who are nearby and can provide equally useful information. You can use one person to lead you to another and the personal referral is the best kind because it is more likely to get you inside.

It is important to pursue this chain of referrals because one person will not be able to tell you everything about a certain occupation and you will want to avoid being too influenced by his or her particular biases.

Remember, you must get in to see the people who are doing the work that interests you most. Only by talking personally with the people who are "insiders" will you have a shot at job opportunities when they become available. In contrast, if you depend upon being a name on a piece of paper (such as your resume), you will have about the same odds as the other 500 people who are depending upon their paper credentials to carry them through.

Talk to anyone who conceivably might help you, especially secretaries — often they present the first wall you must cross. Get information from them about when the boss is available. Tell them what your interests are; show enthusiasm and eventually you will meet the people you have been waiting to see.

(4) Job Interviews and Resumes

We have not talked about developing a resume and what happens once you are having a job interview because there are numerous books and workbooks available which treat this subject well. We are talking about what you must do before a resume and job interview become necessary. If you do not create your own career and evaluate your potential employers with care, then resumes and job interviews will be largely futile efforts.

If you want to read a fuller explanation of this theory of job hunting, pay particular attention to What Color Is Your Parachute? by Richard Bolles. * Pages two through thirty-three tell you what is wrong with the way that most people look for jobs and the rest of the book tells you the right ways to go about the process.

Reading this book carefully, you will discover that Bolles stresses the importance of a "proposal" as a vehicle which is far superior to a resume. He explains in some detail how you can develop a proposal which describes what you believe you can contribute to an organization after you have done the necessary research on the organization and have conducted the necessary information seeking interviews.

Much of the direction of this entire exercise was inspired by What Color Is Your Parachute?

---

*Richard Bolles, *What Color Is Your Parachute? A Practical Manual for Job-Hunters & Career Changers*. Berkeley, Calif.: Ten Speed Press, 1973. (Box 4310, Berkeley, Ca. 94704).

Part Three: *The Inquiring Reporter*

The following questions are suggested as a framework for your research on a particular occupation. The questions are phrased to be asked of a person who is working in the occupation you are studying.

Occupation under study: ....

Name of employing organization: ....

    Address: ....

        ....

Name of person interviewed: ....

    Job title: ....

Suggested Questions:

1. How long have you worked in this job? ....

2. How long have you worked for this organization? ....

3. What are your major responsibilities? ....

    ....

    ....

    ....

4. What are the criteria on which your performance is evaluated?

    ....

    ....

    ....

5. Who is your immediate supervisor? ....

    What is his (or her) title? ....

    Who is his (or her) immediate superior? ....

    What is the superior's title? ....

6. What do you perceive to be the major rewards of the job? ....

    ....

    ....

    ....

7. What do you like most about this work? ....

....

....

8. What are the major frustrations in this job? ....

....

....

9. What are the most frequently recurring problems? ....

....

....

10. Is your job better or worse now than it was a few years ago? ....
    Why? ....

....

....

11. What job in the organization would you prefer above your own?

....

12. Do you have any long-range goals in this kind of work? ....

....

13. If you were to resign from this job, what kind of work would you seek?

....

14. What advice would you give to a young man coming into a job like yours?

....

....

15. Would your advice be any different for a young woman? ....

....

....

Part Four: *Interim Jobs*

A good Interim Job should meet all of the following criteria:

      (a) Little or no qualifications required

      (b) Availability

      (c) Exposure to many different people in a variety of jobs

The 26 jobs noted below generally satisfy all three of the above conditions for most people in most locations.

* * * *

Census Taker: Collecting information which most people consider non-threatening gives you the opportunity to talk with many people about their work.

Opinion Poll Interviewer: Same as above only more so because polls are growing in usage and acceptance.

Commuter Train Conductor: Plenty of opportunity to talk with commuters about their jobs as they ride to and from work.

News Reporter: Regardless of how small or insignificant your press card may be, it gives you valuable access to many people in the working world.

Retail Store Clerk: Especially in a book store, cigar store, clothing store or drug store, people often have time to chat and provide insights into the work they do.

Cab Driver: Constant chances to pick up valuable clues about various professions, businessmen often chat with cab drivers.

Marketing Research Interviewer: Obtain product preference information and, in the process, ask people about their work situations.

Bartender: Perhaps the ideal opportunity to listen to people when they are relaxed.

Museum Guard: Chance to observe and talk to a variety of people.

Waitress in a Singles Bar: The clientele is close to your own age and likely to have numerous insights into the good and bad aspects of a range of work situations.

Hospital Orderly: Opportunity to talk to a truly captive audience.

Security Guard: If you can overcome the barrier of the uniform, there are plenty of people to talk with.

Golf Caddie: People who have the time and inclination to play this game usually have rather interesting professions and often depend on you for conversation.

Short Order Cook: People are more agreeable when they are being fed and you would probably serve them at lunchtime, between halves of their working day.

Retail Credit Investigator: Finding out credit-risk information about people can involve gathering a lot of other information that may help you in later job-hunting.

Comparison Shopper: You get exposure to a lot of people by visiting a number of different stores each day.

Model: A pleasant way to get attention from people and gather information for your future career.

Receptionist: You are the first line of exposure to people who visit the organization. Choose an organization inhabited by employees or customers whom you would like to meet.

Employment Agency Interviewer: A good way to learn about job availability from an insider's vantage point.

Real Estate Agent: Spend the time to get a license and you will be exposed to many people who will need your help and will have time to talk while they are riding to and from houses or apartments.

Photographer's Helper: People like to have their pictures taken and do not mind talking with the photographer on a variety of subjects.

Travel Agent: Everyone travels at one time or another and very often do so for the purpose of looking for a new job.

Advertising Space Salesperson: Sell space for newspapers, radio, trade magazines, TV, to a wide range of organizations.

Mail Carrier: A vital service and an opportunity to visit homes, businesses, stores, government offices, churches, hospitals, etc.

Handyman: Offer a maintenance or repair service for homeowners and you will have a chance to visit with many people about their jobs, etc.

Temporary Office Worker: An all-purpose Interim Job available in metropolitan areas; the all-time champ for giving you an opportunity to sample a variety of work situations because you work for a few days or weeks for various employers in different settings.

Section V:

APPENDIX

Appendix:

Selected List of Directories

GENERAL
College Placement Annual. College Placement Council, Bethlehem, Pa. (annual)
Occupational listings of employers with data about recruiting director and types of positions offered, major fields of study desired, etc.; employers consist largely of medium to large private companies.
Directory of Scholarly and Research Publishing Opportunities. Academic Media, Orange, N.J., (1971).
A guide to academic publishing in the humanities, social sciences, and science-technology areas; names, addresses, and requirements of each publication.
Research Centers Directory. Gale Research, Detroit, Mich. 2nd Edition, (1965).
A guide to university-sponsored and non-profit research organizations which have research programs in agriculture, business, conservation, education, engineering and technology, government, law, life sciences, mathematics, area studies, physical and earth sciences, social sciences, and humanities.
Washington III. Potomac Books, Washington, D.C., (1971).
A comprehensive directory of the nation's capital; names & addresses of govt. agencies, media, banks, medical services, cultural institutions, foundations, & all other employment institutions.

ADVERTISING
The Standard Directory of Advertisers. National Register Publishing Co., New York, N.Y. (annual)
Lists 17,000 companies, key personnel, advertising agencies they use, budget, and media used.
The Standard Directory of Advertising Agencies. National Register Publishing Co., New York, N.Y. (annual)
Lists 4,000 advertising agencies, their key personnel, and names of accounts.

ART & MUSEUMS
American Art Directory. 44th edition, Jacques Cattell Press, R. R. Bowker, Co., New York, New York, 1970.
Extensive lists of the museums, art schools, and art associations in the U.S. and Canada, with names of officials, data on special collections, etc.
The Official Museum Directory. American Assoc. of Museums, Washington, D.C., 1971.
6,600 entries of museums in the U.S. arranged geographically, with cross-listing by type of museum.
Private Foundations Active in the Arts. Editors of Washington International Arts Letter, Washington, D.C., 1970.
Over 630 foundations which relate to the arts and humanities, names and addresses of officials in each.
International Directory of Arts. Published by Deutsche Zentraldruckerei, Berlin, Germany, 1971-72.
Names of art museums and galleries in foreign countries.

BUSINESS

Investment Companies. Wiesenberger Services, Inc., New York, N.Y., 1973.
   Detailed descriptive information about mutual funds and other investment companies in the U.S.A.

Hotel and Motel Redbook. American Hotel Assoc. Directory Corp., New York, N.Y. (annual)
   Complete listings of all hotels and motels in the U.S.; includes address, name of manager, etc.

Poor's Register of Corporation Directors and Executives. Standard and Poor's Corp., New York, N.Y. (annual)
   A directory of all major corporations, their directors and executives in the U.S.

Professional Guide to Public Relations. Prentice Hall, Englewood Cliffs, N.J., 1971.
   Lists 514 public relations services with names and addresses of firms, key personnel; types of firms include clipping bureaus; literary; mailing, radio and TV, P.R. services; media directories; motion picture distributors, etc.

COMMUNICATIONS

Audio/Visual Marketplace. R. R. Bowker Co., New York, N.Y., 1970.
   A directory of the audio-visual industry, listing producers and distributors, equipment, services and organizations, conventions, film festivals, etc.

SOURCE Catalog (Communications). Swallow Press, Chicago, Ill., 1971.
   Names and addresses of non-traditional organizations and projects in mass media, art, music, theater, and many other forms of communication.

1974 Broadcasting Yearbook. Broadcast Publications, Washington, D.C. (annual)
   Complete list of all TV and AM-FM radio stations in the U.S. and Canada, including addresses and telephone numbers, licenses and owners, names of representatives.

CONSERVATION-ENVIRONMENT

The Conservation Directory. National Wildlife Federation, Washington, D.C., 1974.
   A directory of a wide variety of governmental, private, and other conservation organizations, classified by state and purpose; includes names of leaders of these organizations, and description of their purposes.

Directory of Consumer Protection and Environmental Agencies. Academic Media, Orange, N.J., 1973.
   State-by-state listings of governmental and private organizations involved in consumer protection and environmental protection, with names of key personnel.

NFEC Directory of Environmental Information Sources. National Foundation for Environmental Control, Boston, Mass. 2nd Edition, 1972.
   Government agencies, legislative commissions, citizens organizations, professional organizations, trade associations, and educational institutions concerned with environmental protection.

EDUCATION

Patterson's American Education. Educational Directories, Inc., Mt. Prospect, Ill. (annual)
   Names of all public and private schools in the U.S.; names of officials, data on each school.

Private Schools, Porter Sargent, Boston, Mass. (annual)
   Names and descriptions of all private schools in U.S.; key officials.

Private Independent Schools. Bunting & Lyon, Wallingford, Conn., 1969.
   Names, addresses, and descriptions of boarding schools, day schools, and military schools.

1974 Directory of Counseling Services. International Association of Counseling Services, Washington, D.C.
   Directory of counseling services approved by I. A. C. S., services offered, names of directors, kinds of professionals on the staff, etc.

Comparative Guide to American Colleges, 73-74. Harper & Row, New York, N.Y.
Description of four-year colleges in the U.S., with indexes by state, religious affiliation, selectivity, and number of degrees granted in various fields.

Directory for Exceptional Children. Porter Sargent, Boston, Mass., 1972.
Lists private residential schools and day schools, as well as treatment centers for the emotionally disturbed and socially maladjusted children.

Early Childhood Education Directory. R. R. Bowker Co., New York, N.Y. 1st edition, 1971.
A guide to approximately 2,000 schools devoted to the educational interests of pre-school children; includes nursery schools, day care, head starts, Montessori, and others.

1973-74 Directory of Alternative Schools. New Schools Exchange, P. O. Box 820, St. Paris, Ohio 43072.
Listings of alternatives, free, experimental, and other non-traditional schools by state, including description of the school's purpose and activities.

FOREIGN

Schools Abroad. Porter Sargent, Boston, Mass. 2nd edition, 1967.
Private elementary and secondary schools in various countries outside U.S.A.

Foreign Language Press List. American Council for Nationalities Services, New York, N.Y., 1971.
Detailed listings of foreign language and nationality publications in the U.S.; provides names, addresses, frequency of publication, name of publisher; arranged by language, city, and state.

Directory of American Firms Operating in Foreign Countries. World Trade Academy Press, New York, N.Y., 1969.
Data on more than 3,000 American corporations operating overseas, arranged with geographical cross-references, and categorized by product.

International Literary Marketplace. R. R. Bowker, Co., New York, N.Y., 1971-72.
Firm name, address, phone number, and key personnel of 2,300 active publishers in various countries.

Selective Guide to Overseas Employment. Regents Publishing Co. (division of Simon & Schuster), New York, N.Y., 1968.
Discusses overseas employment requirements, fields, and gives specific information for selected countries in South America, Europe, Africa, Australia, Japan, India, and Philippines.

Your Future In Jobs Abroad. Richard Rosen Press, New York, N.Y., 1968.
Includes lists of American companies that operate in other countries.

American Register of Exporters & Importers. American Register of Exporters/Importers Corp., New York, N.Y., 1971.
Directory of over 30,000 manufacturers, export/import buying agencies, by product class; Also, foreign offices of Chamber of Commerce and U.S. buying agencies.

GOVERNMENT-POLITICS-HISTORY

U.S. Government Organization Manual. Office of Federal Register, General Services Administration, Washington, D.C., 1972-73.
Contains a description and organization chart for every agency and department of the federal government, complete with names of the key officials.

The Municipal Yearbook. International City Management Assoc., Washington, D.C., 1973.
Includes mayors and city officials for most towns and cities in the U.S., plus considerable demographic data.

Encyclopedia of Government Advisory Organizations. Gale Research Co., Detroit, Mich., 1973.
A reference guide to federal agencies, inter-agency, and government-related boards, committees, councils, etc.

The Political Marketplace. Quadrangle Books, New York, N.Y., 1972.
   Names and addresses, by state, of the elected leadership of the nation, the political leadership, and major media outlets.
From Radical Left to Extreme Right. Campus Publishers, 711 N. University Ave., Ann Arbor, Mich. 2nd edition, 1970.
   A bibliography of current periodicals of protest, controversy, advocacy, or dissent.
Directory of Historical Societies and Agencies in the U.S. and Canada, '73-74.
   Joint publication of the American Association for State and Local History (Nashville and Inforonics, Inc. (Maynard, Mass.) ed. by Donna McDonald.
      Names and addresses of historical societies by state.
National Register of Historic Places. U.S. Government Printing Office, Washington, D.C., 1972.
   Name and historic background, by state, of all historic places in the U.S.A.

MUSIC

The Musician's Guide. Music Information Service, New York, N.Y., 1972.
   A complete directory of music associations, competitions, awards, grants, music colleges, libraries, discographies, music festivals, editors, critics, etc., with names of key individuals.
Directory of Music Research Libraries. University of Iowa, Iowa City, Ia., 1970.
   Listing of all music research libraries in the U.S.

SCIENCE

American Council of Independent Laboratories Directory, 1969-1970. American Council of Independent Laboratories, Washington, D.C.
   A guide to the leading testing, research, and inspection laboratories of America, cross-referenced by services offered and geographic location.
Directory of Federal R & D Installations. U.S. Government Printing Office, Washington, D.C., 1971.
   Over 1,000 pages of listings of research and development installations in various states.
International Scientific Organizations. Reference Department, Library of Congress, Washington, D.C., 1962.
   A guide to the library, documentation, and information services of international scientific organizations.

SOCIAL SERVICES

Mental Health Directory. National Clearinghouse for Mental Health Information, U.S. Government Printing Office, Washington, D.C., 1971.
   Geographical listing by state of all mental health agencies in the U.S. and the service they provide.
Invest Yourself. Commission on Voluntary Service and Action, New York, N.Y. (annual)
   A directory of agencies and numerous nonprofit organizations, many of which are church-related, that use volunteers extensively and are engaged in social work missions.
1970 Directory—United Way of America. United Way of America, New York, N.Y.
   Listings of United Funds, Community Chests, and Community Health and Welfare Councils which are members of the United Way of America; includes address and name of the key executive.
Vocations for Social Change. Vocations for Social Change, Canyon, Calif.
   Journal containing information on social change projects, staff openings in existing organizations, national and regional sources of information, and names of individuals to contact.

SOURCE Catalog (Communities/Housing). Swallow Press, Chicago, Ill., 1972.
>   Names and addresses of non-traditional projects in legal work, open housing, city wide organizing, and many others.

Profiles of Involvement. Human Resources Corp., Philadelphia, Pa., (3 volumes) 1972.
>   A summary of hundreds of private corporations and other organizations which are involved in social service projects; descriptions of these projects, and names of people to contact.

WRITING-PUBLISHING-LIBRARY WORK

American Book Trade Directory, 1971-72. R. R. Bowker, Co., New York, N.Y.
>   The standard directory of retail bookstores in the U.S. and Canada, arranged geographically by state and city.

American Library Directory, 1970-71. R. R. Bowker, Co., New York, N.Y. (biennial)
>   Lists public libraries, county and regional systems, college and university libraries, and private libraries; includes names of key personnel and addresses.

Directory of Special Libraries and Information Centers. Gale Research Corp., Detroit, Mich., (2 volumes) 1968.
>   Volume I: Special libraries listed include those in colleges and universities, branches of public libraries concentrating on one group of subjects, company, government, and nonprofit sponsored libraries; Volume II lists names of personnel.

Literary Market Place, 1973-74. R. R. Bowker, Co., New York, N.Y.
>   Names, titles, addresses, and phone numbers for all publishers in the U.S.; includes book publishers classified by kinds of books, magazine publishers, newspaper publishers; also includes advertising agencies, public relations firms, and other communications industry services.

1974 Ayer Directory. Ayer Press, Philadelphia, Pa.
>   Lists newspapers, magazines, and trade publications published in the U.S., Canada, Bermuda, Panama, Philippines; cross-indexed.

The Writer's Handbook. The Writer, Inc., Boston, Mass. (annual)
>   Lists over 2,000 magazines, newspapers, and other publications to which individuals can submit manuscripts for sale.

Writers and Artists Yearbook. The Writer, Inc., Boston, Mass., 1974.
>   A directory for writers, artists, playwrights, writers for film, radio, TV, photographers, and composers.

Worldwide Directory of Federal Libraries. Academic Media, Orange, N.J., 1973.
>   Directory of all federal libraries, categorized by federal agency, with names of key personnel.

Literary and Library Prizes. R. R. Bowker, Co., New York, N.Y. 8th edition, 1973.
>   A directory of International, American, British, and Canadian prizes for literary and library work; descriptions of criteria for each prize.

The Standard Periodical Directory. Oxbridge Publishing Co., New York, N.Y. 2nd edition, 1967.
>   Names, addresses, editors, and descriptions of industrial, business, farm, medical, legal, general interest, government, arts and humanities, and trade journals; also newsletters, house organs, financial services, and others.

1973 Editor and Publisher International Yearbook. Editor & Publisher Co., New York, N.Y.
>   Encyclopedia of the newspaper industry; listing, by state, of all U.S. and foreign daily and weekly newspapers, key management personnel, advertising rates; also, syndicates, press clubs, foreign correspondents, journalism schools, and other relevant information.

Appendix:

BIBLIOGRAPHY

Bolles, Richard N. *What Color Is Your Parachute? A Practical Manual for Job-Hunters & Career-Changers*. Berkeley, California: Ten Speed Press, 1972.

Borow, Henry (ed.). *Career Guidance For a New Age*. Boston: Houghton-Mifflin, 1973.

Calvert, Robert, Jr. *Career Patterns of Liberal Arts Graduates*. 2nd ed. Cranston, R.I.: The Carroll Press, 1973.

Carkhuff, Robert R. *The Art of Problem Solving*. Amherst, Mass.: Human Resources Development Press, 1973.

Chase, Stuart. *The Proper Study of Mankind*. New York: Harper, 1948.

Colgate, Craig, Jr. *1974 National Trade and Professional Associations of the U.S.* Washington, D.C.: Columbia Books, 1974.

Crystal, John and Bolles, Richard N. *Where Do I Go From Here With My Life?* New York: Seabury Press, 1974.

Crystal, John. "Clustering of Your Skills." McLean, Va.: Crystal Management Services, 1973 (unpublished material).

Dictionary of Occupational Titles, Volumes I-III. Washington, D.C.: U.S. Department of Labor, 1965, U.S. Government Printing Office.

Drum, David J. and Figler, Howard E. *Outreach in Counseling*. New York: Intext Educational Publishers, 1973.

Dunphy, Philip W., ed. *Career Development for the College Student*. 2nd ed. Cranston, R.I.: The Carroll Press, 1973.

Figler, Howard E. "Basic Job Satisfaction and the Need for Life Counseling." *Journal of College Placement*, February-March, 1972.

Figler, Howard E. "How to do Career Counseling When the Student Offers You Only One Hour of His Time." *Journal of College Placement*, Fall issue, 1974.

Figler, Howard E. "Path: A Vocational Exploration Program for Liberal Arts Students." *Journal of College Placement*, October-November, 1973.

Goodman, Paul. *Growing Up Absurd*. New York: Vintage Books, 1956.

Hodge, R. W.; Siegel, P. M., and Rossi, P. H. "Occupational Prestige in the U.S., 1925-1963." (in) *Class, Status, and Power*, R. Bendix and S. M. Lipset (eds.), 2nd edition. New York: The Free Press, 1966.

Hoffer, Eric. *Ordeal of Change*. New York: Harper and Row, 1963.

Hopke, William (ed.). *Encyclopedia of Careers and Vocational Guidance*. Revised Edition, Volumes I and II. Chicago: Ferguson Publishing Co., 1972.

Irish, Richard, *Go Hire Yourself an Employer*. New York: Doubleday, Anchor Books, 1973.

Jones, John E. and Pfeiffer, J. William (eds.). *1973 Annual Handbook for Group Facilitators*, "Traditional American Values: Intergroup Confrontation." Iowa City, Iowa: University Associates.

Katz, Martin R. "The Name and Nature of Vocational Guidance." (in) *Career Guidance for a New Age*, Henry Borow (ed.). Boston: Houghton-Mifflin, 1973.

Katz, Martin R. *Decisions and Values: A Rationale for Secondary School Guidance*. New York: College Entrance Examination Board, 1963.

Katz, Martin R. "A Model of Guidance for Career Decision Making." *Vocational Guidance Quarterly*, Volume 15, 1966.

Larrabee, Harold A. *Reliable Knowledge*. Boston: Houghton-Mifflin, 1945.

Levenstein, Aaron. "Work and Its Meaning in an Age of Affluence." (in) *Career Guidance for a New Age*, Henry Borow (ed.). Boston: Houghton-Mifflin, 1973.

Muller, Herbert J. *Uses of the Past*. New York: Oxford University Press, 1953.

Nutter, Carolyn F. *The Resume Workbook: A Personal Career File for Job Applications*. 4th ed. Cranston, R.I.: The Carroll Press, 1970.

Occupational Outlook Handbook, 1973-74 Edition. Washington, D.C.: U.S. Department of Labor, Bureau of Labor Statistics, Government Printing Office.

Pfeiffer, J. William and Jones, John E. *Structured Experiences for Human Relations Training*. Volume II, "Consensus Seeking: A Group Ranking Task." Iowa City, Iowa: University Associates Press, 1973.

Raths, Louis; Harmin, Merrill, and Simon, Sidney. *Values and Teaching*. Columbus, Ohio: Charles E. Merrill Publishers, 1966.

Rosenberg, Morris. *Occupations and Values*. Glencoe, Ill.: The Free Press, 1957.

Sandman, Peter. *The Unabashed Career Guide*. London: Collier Books, 1969.

Simon, Sidney; Howe, Leland, and Kirschenbaum, Howard. *Values Clarification: A Handbook of Practical Strategies for Teachers and Students*. New York: Hart Publishing Co., 1972.

Slater, Philip. *The Pursuit of Loneliness*. Boston: Beacon Press, 1970.

Super, Donald E. "A Theory of Vocational Development." (in) *The American Psychologist*, 1953.

Super, Donald E. "Vocational Development Theory: Persons, Positions, and Processes." *The Counseling Psychologist*, Volume 1, No. 1, 1969.

Super, Donald, and Crites, J. O. *Appraising Vocational Fitness*, Revised Edition, New York: Harper Brothers, 1962.

Taylor, F. W. "On the Art of Cutting Metals," *Transactions of the American Society of Mechanical Engineers*. 1907, Volume 28.

Teal, Everett A. (ed.). *The Occupational Thesaurus* (Volumes I and II). Bethlehem, Pa.: Lehigh University, 1971.

Thorndike, Robert and Hagen, Elizabeth. *Ten Thousand Careers*. New York: John Wiley & Sons, 1959.

NOTES

Use the following pages to record notes which do not readily fit into any of the exercises; such as — assignments by your group leader; comments on your career prospects by others in your group or outside (parents, faculty, counselors, peers); and your private thoughts about your future career.

NOTES

NOTES

NOTES